Colmán of Cloyne

CORK STUDIES IN IRISH HISTORY

Colmán of Cloyne
A Study

Paul MacCotter

FOUR COURTS PRESS

Set in 11 pt on 15 pt Garamond for
FOUR COURTS PRESS LTD
7 Malpas Street, Dublin 8, Ireland
e-mail: info@four-courts-press.ie
http://www.four-courts-press.ie
and in North America by
FOUR COURTS PRESS
c/o ISBS, 920 N.E. 58th Avenue, Suite 300, Portland, OR 97213.

A catalogue record for this title
is available from the British Library.

ISBN 1–85182–793–5

Printed in Great Britain
by MPG Books, Bodmin, Cornwall.

Contents

Contents

Abbreviations

A Clon	D. Murphy (ed.), *The Annals of Clonmacnoise* (Dublin, 1896).
AFM	J. O'Donovan (ed.), *Annála Roighachta Éireann: Annals of the Kingdom of Ireland by the Four Masters* (7 vols, Dublin, 1848–51).
ALC	W.M. Hennessy (ed.), *The Annals of Loch Cé* (2 vols, London, 1871).
AI	S. Mac Airt (ed.), *The Annals of Inisfallen* (Dublin, 1951).
A Tig	W. Stokes (ed.), *The Annals of Tigernach* (2 vols, reprinted Lampeter, 1993).
AU	W.M. Hennessy and B. MacCarthy (ed.), *Annála Uladh: The Annals of Ulster* (4 vols, Dublin, 1887–1901).
CS	W.M. Hennessy (ed.), *Chronicon Scotorum* (London, 1866).
CGH	M.A. O'Brien (ed.), *Corpus Genealogiarum Hiberniae*, i (Dublin, 1962).
CSH	P. Ó Riain (ed.), *Corpus Genealogiarum Sanctorum Hiberniae* (Dublin, 1985).
FAI	J.N. Radnor (ed.), *Fragmentary Annals of Ireland* (Dublin, 1978).
JCHAS	*Journal of the Cork Historical and Archaeological Society.*
JRSAI	*Journal of the Royal Society of Antiquaries of Ireland.*
MIA	S. Ó hInnse (ed.), *Miscellaneous Irish Annals* (Dublin, 1947).
PRC	Paul MacCotter and Kenneth Nicholls (eds), *The pipe roll of Cloyne (Rotulus Pipae Clonensis)*, (Midleton, 1996).
PRIA	*Proceedings of the Royal Irish Academy.*
ZCP	*Zeitschrift für Celtische Philologie.*

CHAPTER ONE

Introduction

Colmán mac Léinín, poet, monk, and saint, is credited with the foundation of the monastery of Cluain Uama, Cloyne, Co. Cork. In the twelfth century this important church became the seat of a bishopric under the new 'reforming' dispensation and so, in turn, Colmán became the patron of the diocese of Cloyne. It is the belief of one important scholar[1] that no life of the saint was ever written, and it is certain that none has come down to us today, but, given the vagaries of Irish history and the certain destruction of so much source material, can we really be confident of this? Colmán was certainly a saint of sufficient importance to justify such a life, as will be demonstrated in the present study, and we may note that lives of two minor saints within the diocese of Cloyne do survive, apparently mere accidents of history and in no way representative of the importance of the cults concerned.[2]

The lack of an existing life may go some way to explaining why surprisingly little has been written about this saint in recent times, and one has to go back to James Coleman's paper on the saint, which appeared in 1910, to find the most recent biographical account of any substance written on Colmán, and which included a survey of what little had preceded it.

The modern reader will be aware of the substantial improvement in the standard of Early Irish ecclesiastical historiography over the past century, more especially within the last generation, and, with this in mind, a revisitation of the subject of St Colmán is long overdue. Perhaps a further good reason to desire such a revisit is the substantial amount of attention lavished on the patron of the neighbouring diocese, Finbarr of Cork, in the last generation, mostly due to the extensive work of

1 Ó Riain, 1997a, 89. 2 These were Molaca of Templemolaga and Findchú of Brigown (O'Keeffe; Stokes, 1890, 84–98).

Professor Pádraig Ó Riain of University College, Cork.[3] An end to this local imbalance is required.

The present work has firstly assembled all materials relevant to Colmán, before going on to subject this evidence – in chronological order – to the methodologies developed by the leading authorities on the period, in particular Etchingham, Ó Corráin, Ó Riain and Sharpe. My particular interest in the subject of the present study derives from his uniqueness among his fellows, for it has long seemed to me that Colmán mac Léinín is quite exceptional in comparison to the run-of-the-mill early Irish saint for reasons which will become clear in the present study. In connexion with my dependence upon the authorities listed above, it should be noted that, unsurprisingly perhaps in light of the nature of the period under scrutiny, these authorities often differ in both methodology and result. In such cases my aim has been to make full use of all available methodology. All conclusions reached are, of course, entirely my own unless otherwise stated, as must inevitably be any errors which may be found in the present work.

The picture which emerges from this work essentially confirms the core of the received history of Colmán mac Léinín, while debunking much accreted myth. New evidence of the life and times of the saint himself is adduced, while the history of his cult and of his ecclesiastical foundations is revealed as fully as the fragmentary sources allow. This history is intimately involved with, and firmly placed in the context of, the socio-political realities of the period from Colmán's life until the time of the Anglo-Norman conquest.

We find abundant evidence that Colmán mac Léinín does indeed appear to have existed – in clear contrast to the picture which emerges of Finbarr of Cork, for whom early evidence is virtually non-existent.[4] Colmán's period stands at the very beginning of written Irish history, and the study of his life and times is all the more exciting for that. Native, most likely, to south eastern Co. Limerick or the adjacent parts of Tipperary; poet, scholar, and later monk; during his sixth century life he had some kind of relationship with Cairpre Crom, overking of Munster, who

---

3 Ó Riain, 1977a, 1985, 1994, 1997a. **4** Ó Corráin 1985a; Ó Riain 1997a, 89.

beneficed him with Cloyne and other lands, and in whose service Colmán cursed his (Cairpre's) enemies. After the saint's death the relationship between Cairpre's descendants and Colmán's cult appears to have been one of mutual dependence and, by the twelfth century (and probably much earlier), the cult mirrors the extent of the area of dominance of Cairpre's descendants, the Uí Chaím, which in turn appears to represent the area of the *paruchia* of Colmán's foundation of Cluain Uama. It was this area which subsequently became the template for the diocese of Cloyne.

This is perhaps the best place to advert briefly to my stance on the general question of the form or model of the Early Irish Church, given that substantial agreement on this question among scholars of the period still lies some way in the future, and indeed the subject remains controversial. It is especially important that this issue be addressed in this Introduction for the following reasons. There is a paucity of evidence surviving from this early period in relation to the church of Cloyne. The methodology of interpretation to be applied to this evidence and the general model of church organization to be used to provide a skeleton on which the evidence will hang obviously has a direct bearing on the resultant conclusions which will be drawn; therefore some explanation of my position on these questions is necessary here.

The survival rate for source material over the period of the Early Irish Church is geographically highly uneven. As ill-luck would have it, south Munster or Desmond (*Desmuma*) is particularly poorly served in this context. This lack of evidence can be partly compensated for by studying the evidence from those parts of Ireland better served by the sources and applying the insights so gained into the structure of society to the interpretation of the modicum of evidence surviving for our area of study, bearing in mind the marked cultural and religious homogeneity of Early Gaelic Ireland. Of course this methodology is predicated on the assumption that studies exist of sufficient competence to allow such a societal framework to be identified. In the last two decades or so the study of Early Ireland and particularly of the Early Irish Church has shown a state of satisfactory development after many decades of inertia. While the level of agreement among leading scholars on the shape of the society of this period is perhaps not as great as one would like I believe that recent studies of the period, in particular that of Dr Colmán Etchingham of NUI Maynooth (to whom the present study owes much), offer an image of early medieval Ireland which accords better with the evidence than anything heretofore. While I have drawn inspiration from many sources in the course of the present study I must acknowledge an especial debt to this work. The school of thought of which Etchingham's work represents the present pinnacle is, of course, still 'young' and, in the nature of such things, is far from meeting with complete acceptance now. I believe, however, that this will come in due course and, given that this view is the polar opposite of the 'traditional' picture, one really does not have the option of being a 'hurler on the ditch' in this matter. I have made clear where I stand on this question. The following account is not meant to be a comprehensive summary of the question of the Early Irish Church, for the subject is extremely complicated and difficult of treatment, but rather a brief *resumé* for the purposes of the present study.

The traditional picture of the Early Irish Church as held by scholars was one where the original Patrician territorial diocesan structure was superseded in the seventh century by one where the principal organizational mode of the Church took the form of large monasteries ruled by an abbot which held sway over extensive and often dispersed territories or *paruchiae,* with the episcopacy reduced to virtual irrelevancy, and which saw a degenerate laicization over several centuries from the early pinnacle of monastic 'purity'.[5] This superficial and impressionistic picture presented many problems of unintegrated evidence.

The picture presented instead by recent scholarship is at once more simple and more complex.[6] It has been suggested that from at least the mid-seventh century onwards – when the survival rate of documentation improves markedly – the Irish Church is found using a flexible model of church government in which a single, eclectic system embraced episcopal, abbatial, and temporal ('coarbial') authority in a variety of possible permutations. There is evidence that the major church centres were not

5 Etchingham 1994, passim; Etchingham 1999, 12–21. **6** Most of the discussion in the following paragraphs is based on Etchingham 1999, passim, and Ó Corráin 1981a, passim.

simply monastic but also episcopal and coarbial in nature. Abbots might also be bishops but both roles could exist separately in the same centre as could the third function of church government, that of territorial lordship when the leadership of a church could be held by a lay administrator or coarb – often hereditary – acting vicariously, as it were, in his church's interest. Terminological flexibility appears to have been the norm. Not alone is there evidence for the continued existence throughout the early period of tiers of territorial episcopacy but even of territorial archepiscopacy exercising metropolitan authority. In most cases such territorial bishoprics were seated in centres traditionally seen as monasteries but which should more realistically be seen as important church centres which may or may not have included a cenobitic element, and which may indeed have more resembled the 'minster' of Anglo-Saxon England than the traditional image of the 'Celtic' monastery (see 9.2).

Turning to the question of the nature of territorial lordship exercised by such Irish church centres, again the traditional picture of the dispersed monastic *paruchia* or *fairche* has been found wanting. In some cases at least the *paruchia* has been shown to correspond to an episcopal sphere of pastoral jurisdiction and in general, if not exclusively, would appear to have been geographically cohesive, while being subject to the triple model of leadership referred to already. While the principal presiding officer in a *paruchia* could be an abbot or lay *princeps* the general trend of the evidence suggests that most if not all *paruchiae* would have had a resident bishop – who may also have held the abbacy – or even over-bishop and the temptation to equate *paruchia* with the same function as the later diocese is strong, even if the evidence is complex and not always in agreement. Indeed, the use of monastic terminology in general by the Early Irish Church indicates a range of semantic meaning well beyond and outside of the strict sense usually applied to such terminology and the interpretation of such terms should be approached with caution. There is evidence that *paruchiae* may have corresponded to and been influenced by the same forces affecting secular polities. As to the term *familia* or its native equivalent, *muinter*, this might be used to 'denote either the community of an individual church or, by extension, those attached to an associated group of churches'.7

Another intriguing element of the interpretation of the evidence suggests that while the entire population was nominally Christian only those populations resident on church land, i.e. in the Church's sphere of secular lordship, were fully in receipt of pastoral ministry, in return for which various rents and services were offered. Often such residents were members of what has been described as 'a paramonastic elite' of laypersons living lives under the direction of various forms of religious rule, some at least of whom could be described under the general term *manaig,* which, while having several shades of meaning, generally refers to those resident under the Church's secular lordship.[8]

All of this of course applies only to the period after the mid-seventh century. The formative years of the Irish Church are much less understood due to the paucity of evidence. One intriguing possibility is that the pattern of secular church lordship evidenced from the seventh century onwards, where distinct *tuatha* or smaller parcels of lands are owned by the Church in a scattered and random pattern across the landscape, may reflect an earlier period when Christians were a minority in a pagan land and thus preserve an outline of the lands of the earliest Christian communities. Were these early communities therefore operating under ecclesiastical lordship and thus 'of the world but not in the world'?[9]

I am indebted to several people for invaluable assistance in the course of the present study. Professor Donnchadh Ó Corráin of UCC kindly read the manuscript, was most helpful with advice on various aspects of the study, and most helpfully provided modern translations of Colmán's poems (Appendix C). Professor Pádraig Ó Riain of UCC also generously furnished advice and helped provide research material difficult of access as well as reading the manuscript. Mr Kenneth Nicholls of UCC was also of assistance in several ways and I must also acknowledge the support of Mr Tim Cadogan of Cork County Library, the ever helpful staff of Q-1 in the Boole Library, UCC, and very especially Fr Robert Forde of Fermoy. As always, all conclusions (and mistakes, if such there be), unless otherwise attributed, are entirely my own.

7 Etchingham 1999, 129.   8 Ibid., 363–453.   9 I owe this concept to a discussion with Mr Kenneth Nicholls.

CHAPTER TWO

The historiography of Colmán

Before turning to the actual evidence for the life of Colmán it is first necessary to identify and eliminate those errors in the historiographical record concerning the saint. Such accretions of inaccuracy have arisen slowly over many centuries, like stalactites in a limestone cavern, and are themselves of interest in illuminating the attitudes to the saint through the centuries as expressed in hagiography, and will be examined in more detail below (7.3, 7.5). It suffices for the present to identify what is false in preparation for our work in the next chapter.

2.1 The received picture

The received picture of Colmán as represented in twentieth-century hagiography is based on a number of published accounts which appeared between the middle of the nineteenth century and early in the twentieth. The salient points of these, beginning with the fullest account and avoiding repetition, follows.

- Colman of Cloyne, Saint (522–600), was the son of Lenin, who, according to his pedigree in the Book of Leinster, was ninth in descent from Mogh Nuadat, king of Munster, AD 166. His birthday is stated in the Martyrology of Tamlacht to have been 15 October, and the year, which is not exactly ascertained, is believed to have been 522.

- He was brought up in heathenism, and adopted the profession of bard, which required a special education. There were several degrees of rank in it; and to reach the highest twelve years of study were necessary. On completing his education, he was attached to the court of the king of Cashel, and his duties there may be inferred from the fol-

lowing ancient description of the order generally: 'They were historian as well as poets: it was their duty to record the deeds of the kings,
chieftains, and heroes; to describe their battles and victories; to register the genealogies and privileges of noble families, together with
the bounds and limits of their lands and territories.' He was engaged
in these important duties until somewhere about the forty-eighth
year of his age.

• In 570 a dispute as to the succession to the throne of Cashel (or
Munster) took place between two relatives, Aodh Dubh and Aodh
Caomh. To prevent the usual recourse to war, a meeting was arranged
between the rival candidates, at which St Brendan of Clonfert was
present with the son of Lenin; and by their influence a compromise
was effected, by which Aodh Caomh was acknowledged as king, and
in due course was inaugurated with much ceremony. He was the first
Christian king of Cashel, and though the son of Lenin was the offi-
cial bard, the chief place in the proceedings was taken by St Brendan,
apparently because it was appropriate that a Christian ecclesiastic
should install a Christian king. During the proceedings circumstances
let to the discovery of the shrine of Ailbhe of Emly, which had been
stolen; but had fallen into a lake, the thieves having been drowned,
probably when crossing it. The son of Lenin was one of those who
found it; and then Brendan said it was not right that the hands which
had held this sacred relic should be defiled henceforth (that is, by the
heathen observances); hence it was that the son of Lenin offered himself to God and Brendan, and Brendan blessed him and changed his
name.

• The adoption of Christianity, however, made it necessary for him to
resign his office; and as this implied the loss of his livelihood, he
acquainted the king with his difficulties, who granted him in perpe-
tuity a remission of the tribute or rent which was due from his lands
to the kings of Cashel, conferring the same favour on St Brendan also.

• The name given to him by St Brendan on his reception into the
Christian Church was Colman, which is the diminutive of Colum,

the equivalent of the Latin *columbus*, a dove. No less than 209 saints named Colman are enumerated in the book of Leinster, to the immense perplexity of the student of history.

- On becoming a Christian, Colman went to the school of St Jarlath of Tuam to acquaint himself more fully with Christian doctrine; after this the next notice we meet with of him is as engaged in preaching to the heathen population in the east of the county of Cork. He is described as then a 'religious and holy presbyter, who afterwards became a famous bishop.' Here a family connected with the reigning prince of the Deise, in the present county of Waterford, came under his influence, and becoming Christians presented their child for baptism. Colman baptised him and named him Declan, ordering, at the same time, that 'he should be carefully reared, and when he reached his seventh year given in charge to a Christian teacher, if one could be found'. This was the well-known St Declan.

- Colman is stated by Dr O'Donovan to have been present at the great assembly of Drumceat, which took place in 590; but the passage to which he refers from a poem of Colman quoted in the account of the assembly does not assert that he was present.

- Of further incidents which occurred between this period and his death, which took place on 24 November 600, ten years after, we have no documentary evidence; but the connection of many places in the counties of Cork and Limerick with his name at this day proves the reality of his labours.

- His earliest settlement appears to have been at Cloyne, Cluain Uama, the lawn of the cave. The cathedral and round tower are situated on a limestone eminence in the midst of the valley, surrounded by rich meadows. In the rock is the cave extending in various branches underground to a great distance, from which the town derives its name. Here it is supposed Colman took up his abode as a place of security, and the remains of his primitive oratory, known as Colman's Chapel, were still to be seen in 1813.

- Six of Colman's sisters formed a small community in accordance with the practice of the old Irish Church; this was known as 'the daughters of Lenin,' and their church, Cill Inghen Lenin, has given its name to the well-known Killiney Hill, near Dun Laoghaire, Co. Dublin, where its ruins may still be seen.

- His feast day is 24 November, at which the Calendar of Oengus describes him as 'Mac Lenini the Vehement'.[1]

- Towards the close of his earthly pilgrimage, hearing of the fame of the school of Lough Eirce, he (Colmán) wished, though himself a master in the paths of perfection, to visit this monastery and enrol his name among the disciples of St Finbarr.[2]

- St Colman was sometimes named Mitine, whence it may be inferred that he was a native of Muscrighe Mitine, now called Muskerry, in the County Cork. Amongst other works which it is probable were composed by St Colman, one is particularly mentioned, viz., a metrical 'Life of St Senan of Iniscarthy' [sic] writen in Irish in a very elegant style.[3]

- St Colman wrote an Irish poem of five quatrains in honour of St Brendan of Clonfert.[4]

Items listed above are representative of the substance of what has been written about Colmán. The longevity of historical error is a wellknown phenomenon and a great comfort to the lazy historian. The picture presented above continues to be disgorged as the accurate history of our subject to the very present day. Hopefully, the present study will finally consign this picture to its rightful place.

2.2 *Errors in the received picture*

Some of this picture can be immediately discarded as unhistorical and this erroneous material disposed of.

1 Olden.   2 Coleman, 12.   3 Lanigan, ii, 213.   4 Coleman, 13.

The story of Colmán's conversion at the dispute between the two Aodh's can be traced to an eleventh- or twelfth-century piece of Dalcassian propaganda which cleverly alters a much older account of Colmán's patronage by an early Eóghanacht king of Munster and, as it stands, has very little historical value (7.3).

As to Colmán being a presybter and bishop, the early material, such as the martyrologies and the genealogies of the saints and analogous material make no mention of Colmán being in holy orders of any kind and all that can be said with probability is that he was a monk.

The alleged St Jarlath connection first appears in Lynch (1660); it was perpetuated by Lanigan (1822) and is certainly spurious.[5]

Colmán's alleged baptism of Declan is based on an incident in the Latin *Vita Declani* where the infant Declan is indeed baptized by one bishop Colmán, but there is nothing to identify this cleric with our saint. The existence of a cult to a saint of the name in the Ardmore area is well attested and there are no grounds for identifying him with Colmán Mac Léinín.[6]

Turning to Colmán's alleged authorship of material on Saints' Brendan and Senán, in the case of the former, the poem in question is much too modern to be attributed to Colmán's period while the fragment of a Life of Senán of Inis Cathaigh and the Amhra Senáin also attributed to Colmán are also from a much later period.

The tradition that Colmán was among Finbarr's disciples at the latter's school at Loch Eirc (Gougane Barra) is based on a thirteenth- or fourteenth-century redaction of the earlier Irish *Beatha Bharra* where the scribe has turned Mocholmóc of Ross into 'Colman mac Lenyn', yet another accretion of limited historical value.[7]

This leaves only the alleged Mitíne origin of the saint to be dealt with, which can be despatched with equal ease. This is the result of a seventeenth-century scribal error by Michael O'Cleary in his *Genealogiae Regum et Sanctorum Hiberniae*, where he inserts the word 'Mitíne' after

---

5 O'Doherty, ii, 161; Lanigan, ii, 217. 6 Power 1914, 15; *Kilkenny and South East of Ireland Archaeological Journal*, 1856, 40–1. This association, of course, also contradicts the belief that Declan was a pre-Patrician saint. 7 Ó Riain 1994, 115, 149.

Colmán's name at the start of the saint's genealogy.[8] Here the scholar has, perhaps understandably, confused the original genealogy of 'Barrfhind Mitíne' (St Finbarr) with that of Colmán, both patron saints of neighbouring dioceses.

Expunging these errors leaves a core account which will survive scrutiny and which can be supplemented with other material unnoticed by the early commentators, all of which leads us to a picture of a much more interesting saint to that painted heretofore.

---

8 Walsh, 125.

CHAPTER THREE

Colmán's family origins

While the material to be presented below may seem to the non-specialist to be somewhat meagre it represents an abundance of riches in comparison to that pertaining to the great majority of early Irish saints, whose stories must rely solely on what Delehaye and Grosjean have defined as '*les coordonnées hagiographiques*'.[1] These consist of the place and day associated with the saint's cult and his genealogical filiation. Such 'hagiographical co-ordinates' present the most minimal of information and it is rare indeed to find an early saint about whom anything else at all reliable is known – if indeed, even these are reliable. It is hardly surprising then to find one of our modern authorities, Ó Riain, coming to the conclusion that (in paraphrase) most of the Irish saints had no existence as historical persons and were either surrogate pagan deities or localized manifestations of originally single and sometimes genuine cults.[2] We are fortunate indeed with Mac Léinín in that the early materials concerning the saint save us from immersion in such cold waters.

3.1 Genealogies

The earliest source for Mac Léinín, apart from his poetry – to be discussed below (5.2) – is a genealogical snippet from Trinity MS 1298 (*olim* H.2.7) dated by Ó Corráin to the period somewhere between the last quarter of the seventh century to the end of the first quarter of the eighth century.[3] This time period is refreshingly close to the traditional *floruit* of the saint, the second half of the sixth century.

1 As quoted in Ó Riain 1975, 78. 2 Ó Riain 1983, 24–5. 3 Ó Corráin 1998, 198.

Rothrige .i. Eochaid Rothan mac Moga Nuadat ⁊ Oengus Catta da brathair; dia ceniul Mac Lenini ⁊ Mac Duinich hi Fer[aib] Cherda de Araib Cliach

'Rothrige: Eochaid Rothán son of Mug Nuadat and Óengus Catta were two brothers. Of their lineage is MacLéníni and Mac Duinich in Fir Cherda in Ára Cliach.'

A second and somewhat different version of this piece from another source[4] reads:

Coic meic forfhacaib Mog Nuadat .i. Aengus Cata .i. Cata cumal ro-n-alt he ⁊ is uada ita Catráidi ⁊ Eochaid Rothan mac Moga Nuadat a quo Rothraidi …

'Mug Nuadat left five sons i.e. Oengus Catta i.e. Catta the bond-maid reared him and from him descend Cattraige and Eochaid Rothan son of Mug Nuadat from whom Rothrige descend …'

The first of these references can be dated, in all probability, to the last quarter of the seventh century. What strikes one initially about this first fragment is that the later standardized version of the saint's geneal-ogy from the *Corpus*,[5] datable to between the ninth and tenth centuries, is derived from it, albeit having corrupted 'Catta' to 'Carraig' in trans-mission.

Colmán mac Lénin mac Gannchon mac Donola mac Conamla mac Colgan mac Crundmael mac Ailt mac Oengusa Carraig mac Moga Nuadat mac Dergthene

The linkage between both genealogies illustrates to which of the two early peoples mentioned in the second fragment Colmán belonged, namely the Cattraige. This is indicated by Colmán's descent from Oengus

---

4 Ibid., 198n. 5 *CSH* 215.1.

Catta/Carraig, clearly the eponym of Cattraige. It may be noted that MacNeill offers an alternative derivation of the name Cattraige, making it one of the numerous class of animal eponyms in *ríge* by deriving it from the cat.[6] As we shall see below however, it is yet a third derivation that is likely to be more authentic.

3.2 Colmán's people: the Cattraige

We must now turn to what is known of these peoples. The element -*r(a)ige*, from **rígion*, in the name of a people, signifies 'kingdom'. The ancestor name forms the first element. Names in *r(a)ige* are thought to denote very early population groups, as the use of the term becomes progressively rarer during the early centuries of recorded history.[7] Mug Nuadat is an alternative name for Eógan Mór, the eponymous ancestor of the great Eóganacht confederation which ruled Munster from the earliest recorded period until the tenth century. Mug Nuadat means 'slave of Nuadu', the latter being a god of the Celtic pantheon: Nuadu Airgetlám, who is found as Nodens in inscriptions of the Roman period in Britain.[8] All of this emphasizes the very early nature of these references. The actual claim to descent from the mythical and probably divine Mug Nuadat does not need to imply some Eóganacht connection here; it was customary for subject peoples such as the Cattraige to claim descent from mythical early ancestors of their overlords.

Reference to the Cattraige as living among the Fir Cherda in Ára Cliach or Cliu is implicit in the first piece above. Here Fir Cherda is a synonym for the Cerdrige of Tulach Gussa, an early people closely associated with the Eóganacht around Cashel, and whose name suggests that they may have been either hereditary *filid* (poets) or craftsmen.[9] Indeed, the above reference locates both the Cerdrige and that branch of the

---

6 Mac Neill, 81. **7** Ibid., 67. Mr Kenneth Nicholls reminds me that this usage was found in Celtic Gaul as well as in early Ireland among such peoples as the Bituriges and others. **8** Rees and Rees, 31–5, 46, 51, 142; Green, 465, 474, 484. **9** *CGH*, 193.

Cattraige from which Colmán derived in Ára Cliach, a territory which at a minimum comprised the parishes of Kilteely, Knockainy and the barony of Coonagh, essentially the area west and north of Emly, while also including the area around Emly itself.[10] It seems likely that the term may originally have referred to a greater area.

In addition to the above snippet MS 1298 also states that the Cattraige and Rothrige were vassal peoples of the Déisi.[11] These were an important early group of communities settled discontinuously from Waterford through the Tipperary/Limerick borderland up to the area of Limerick itself. More information on this connection comes from the early historico-literary text, *De Causis Torche na nDéisi* (The Expulsion of the Déisi).[12] This tale, datable to the eighth century, purports to tell of the arrival of the Déisi in Munster and of their conquest of lands in what is today southern Tipperary from the Ossrige, events set in the late fifth century. In the account Eithne Uatach, wife of the Eóganacht king of Munster, Óengus mac Nadfraich, and a member of the Déisi, enlists the help of fifty lesser peoples in the conquest of Mag Femin from the Ossrige, among whom were the Cattraige and Rothrige. The tale lists the genealogical origins of all of the fifty peoples. This differs but slightly from that given in the above snippets. Here the Cattraige are said to descend from Glaschat, son of Oilill Ólum – he was, of course, in turn the son of Mug Nuadat – while the Rothrige are derived from Glascach son of Mug Ruith, the legendary druid who was ancestor to the Fir Maige Féne, the eponym people of the territory of Fermoy, Co. Cork. While in this schema the Cattraige are firmly placed with the other peoples said to descend from Oilill Ólum and the Rothrige excluded, the similarity of Glaschat and Glascach once again links them. As always in such texts, the learned clerical author is operating on several levels at once, and one needs to be alert to catch all relevant nuances. The otherwise unattested Mac Duinich of the MS 1298 snippet offers yet another possible Déisi connection. In the published genealogies this name (Duinech) is extremely rare and occurs just once, in a very early section

---

10 Hogan, 33.　11 Dobbs 1939, 309.　12 Meyer 1907, 139.

of the pedigree of the Déisi segment, Uí Óengusa. This segment were eponyms of the later cantred of Ihanegus, located in what is today mid-Co. Waterford around Stradbally and Kilrossanty.[13]

It is not with the Rothrige, however, but with several other minor communities in this area – a palimpsest of different groups intermixed at all levels – that the true antecedents of the Cattraige seem to lie. In the Déisi text the Cattraige are associated with three other groups, each said to descend, as in the case of the Cattraige, from different sons of Oilill Ólum: the Dál Mathrach from Mathrach, Dál maic Cuirp from Mac Cuirp and Dál Didil from Tídell. The descent from Oilill Ólum/Mug Nuadat is again rehearsed in a genealogy of the Síl Ebir. Although this has come down to us in a late – probably eleventh-century – form, it is clearly based on a somewhat older construct.[14] Among the chief peoples of the Síl Ebir as listed in this piece, in addition to the various Eóganacht groups, and the Déisi, the Éili, the Dál Cais and others, are listed the Cattraige along with the three groups linked to them in the Déisi text. The Dál maic Cuirp are again associated with the Cattraige in the tale of the Revolt of the Aithech-Tuatha.[15] In this tale, another branch of the people, the Cattraige Suca, settled along the River Suck in Uí Maine in Connacht, are associated with the Dál Mug Corb, for which read Dál maic Cuirp. Here both are listed among the *aithech-tuatha* or hereditary rent paying tributary peoples of Ireland, said to be of Fir Bolg descent. Another one of these groups, the Dál Didil, are referred to in a ninth century text. This source is the *Tripartite Life of St Patrick*,[16] the relevant section of which begins by featuring Dola (recté Daul), named as the ancestor of the Dál Modula *alias* Corcu Daula, one of the lineages linked (falsely) with Araid, and probably the oldest population group in the Cliu region. After this anecdote follows one concerning one Nena, clearly in some way associated with Daul, from whom the text derives the Menraighe people. This later personage is to be identified with Nóene, another son of Laider the Charioteer in

---

13 *CGH*, 401; Empey 1992, 142–3. 14 *CGH*, 191. 15 Ó Raithbheartaigh, 119. 16 Stokes 1887, 203.

the Araid genealogies.[17] A third anecdote follows immediately, in which Patrick, at a place called Tídell, glossed as the name of a hill, founds a church there, henceforth known as Cill Tidil (now Kilteely). This indirect reference to the Dál Didil is echoed in an annal of 886 concerning Dún Tidall 'in Araid'.[18]

This linkage between Dál Didil and Dál Modula leads to another piece of the puzzle. The Dál Modula were an early *daertuath* or *aithechtuath* of the Eóganacht kings of Cashel, who occur under an earlier synonym of their name in an early eighth-century tract. In this they are called the Corcu Daulai, while yet another early synonym is Daulrige.[19] Here Modula is a hypocoristic form of Daul. A vernacular version of *Betha Bharra* enables us to close the circle. This is the well known section concerning bishop Mac Curp of the Dál Modula, said to have been one of Barra's disciples. Ó Riain has identified the unnamed church of this bishop with Aglishcormack north-west of Emly, based on the relationship between the names Corbmac and Mac Curp, essentially the same name with the elements reversed.[20] This shows that for Dál maic Cuirp we should read Dál Modula. This also gives us an exact location for the Dál Modula. This connection in turn finally leads us to an older schema of genealogical origin for the Cattraige.

As we have seen, the Cattraige are genealogically linked with the Dál Maic Cuirp *alias* Dál Modula. The same linkage – though giving a different common ancestor – occurs in a completely separate and earlier schema. The area along both sides of the Tipperary/Limerick border, variously described by the terms Araid and Cliu with several qualifiers, was home to many different peoples. In addition to the Eóganacht overlords and the Cerdrige, we find several Déisi groups and two sets of peoples, the Dál Coirpre Arad and a group of subservient lordships, one of which was Dál Modula. Their eponymous ancestor, Daul, son of Laider

---

17 *CGH*, 386–7; Ó Raithbheartaigh, 139. The real Araid are Uí Chairpri Arad *alias* Daé Cairpre Arad to whom belong Uí Thréna, Uí Meic Liacc, Dál Cairpri Ditha and Áes Cuilind, linked in by nebulous connexions are Corco Daula and Tácraige and Glasraige Arad, all small lordships subjected to Araid (LL 326g16, Lec. 123va33; I am indebted to Prof. Donnchadh Ó Corráin for this information). **18** *AI*. **19** Ó Raithbheartaigh, 107, 119; *CGH* 386; Hull, 1947, 895. **20** Ó Riain 1997a, 108–9.

the (eponymous) Charioteer, was the eponym of both branches of this people whose descent is recorded in the genealogies down to at least the tenth century. From another son of Laider, Toeca, descend the Tácraige, another lordship subservient to the true Araid, while in one early source the 'Cattraige Arad' are said to descend from Cathnall, father of Laider.[21] This alternative and clearly earlier derivation of the Cattraige from the Araid, one of the oldest of the different population groups in Cliu, is indicative of the antiquity of this same people, again emphasized by the early existence of branches of the Cattraige in at least four provinces for, as we shall see presently, yet other groups are found in the same period in Leinster and Ulster.

An early passage from the Book of Lecan states:

> Cattraige is apportioned some in the Sechtmad, others of them in the Déisi, others of them in Cnámros. They are not allowed [to depart] thence. They remain always with the king of Cashel.[22]

Here we have further evidence of the subservient status of the Cattraige under Cashel. We have already heard of their associations with the Déisi while the Sechtmad (literally 'seventh') was one of the four divisions of Dál Coirpre of Araid. This toponym survived into the Anglo-Norman period as that of a distinct tuath, the 'thwedum of Syachmedh' within which lay the castle of Carrickittle. Ó Riain has persuasively argued that the well known reference from the Book of Armagh to Patrick's Rock at Cashel (*Petram hiCoithrigi hiCaissiul*) is a deliberate ninth-century manipulation of the seventh-century account by Tírechán which in fact referred to 'the rock of the Cattraige at Cashel'. If, as seems likely, Ó Riain is correct here, this provides another very early reference to the Cattraige, one that again imports the sense of a once powerful people recently marginalized. Ó Riain goes on to suggest that the motivation behind Tírechán's reference to the Cattraige here was their association with Dál Modula and the Tácraige, all of whom, he suggests, were related com-

---

21 Ó Raithbheartaigh, 139; *CGH*, 386. **22** Ó Raithbheartaigh, 138.

munities with a hereditary association with the church of Emly, Munster's senior church.[23]

In summary then, Mac Léinín is shown to have been attached to the Cattraige, a people recorded in the earliest sources in several provinces who claimed exalted descent but who appear as one among a group of peoples in a subservient role. More precisely, of the two identifiable subdivisions of this people in vassalage under the kings of Cashel, Mac Léinín is associated with those resident in the area immediately north of Emly, around Kilteely and Carrickittle, as the second group would appear to have been located in Déis Becc (the Ardpatrick/Kilmallock area), an area outside of Ára Cliach.

3.3 The Leinster Connexion

Before leaving the question of Mac Léinín's ethnic origins there is one further association to be noted which confirms his linkage with the Cattraige. The secular background to this association is grounded in the well documented Laigin connexion with much of eastern Munster in the proto-historical period, of which the linkage between the Corcu Lóegde and the Ossrige is only the best known example. The other groups claiming to be originally *forshluinte* of the Laigin were mostly located in what is today Tipperary and eastern Limerick and included both the Araid and Dál Cairpre while a branch of the former is merely one of several segments of these groups to be found settled in Leinster. Another local group with Laigin connexions were the Cerdrige.[24] In light of this phenomenon it is hardly surprising to learn of yet another segment of the Cattraige, this time located in Leinster, which will be referred to presently.

This east Munster – Leinster linkage has a correspondence in hagiography. The cults of several Munster saints, especially those from the area

---

23 Ibid., 138; Hardy, 19b; Ó Riain 1997b, passim. Cf. Ó Riain's description of hereditary itinerant ecclesiastical families (2002, 297, 301) for another possible role for the Cattraige. **24** *CGH* pp. 26, 97; Mac Shamhráin, 53–7, 177; Mac Neill, 94; Byrne 1973, 133.

of the later diocese of Cloyne, are to be found in Leinster. Molaca of Templemolaga is associated with Lann Bechaire (probably at Bremore near Balbriggan) and Templeoge (Tech Molaca), both in Dublin; the Uí Liatháin saints, Gobbán and Cormac, are associated with Kilgobbin, Co. Dublin, and Durrow; Laichtín of the Múscraige is linked with Freshford, Co. Kilkenny; Findchú of Brigown is connected with Cluain Eidhneach (Clonenagh, Co. Laois); Killegar, Co. Wicklow, had a cult of a Finbarr; and lastly in this by no means exhaustive list, we note the dedication of Killiney (Cill Inghen Léinín), Co. Dublin, to the daughters of Léinín and sisters of Colmán. The reverse also obtains to some extent; note the linkage of Abbán of Killabban and Moyarney with the Cloyne churches of Ballyvourney, Coole, Brigown and Kilcrumper.[25] Just as the secular links between east Munster and Leinster have their origins in the proto-historical period before AD 600, so, too, must the hagiographical connexions between these regions derive from these social linkages between the various ethnic groups, linkages which may have continued for some generations after 600. It is in this context then that the dedication of Killiney to Mac Léinín's sisters is probably attributable to the presence of a branch of the Cattraige in Leinster.

Two pieces of evidence indicate this presence. Firstly the early statement that

> Cuthraige (read Cattraige) and Uí Gabhla occupy Uí Chormaic in Laigin, from Áth Cliath to Cuillenn and to Glaise Críche in Cluain Cuada on the side of Laigis to Áth Lethnochta at Slébte till it reaches Uí Bairrche.[26]

From the bounds given in this piece it is clear that the territory in question corresponds to the modern county of Kildare and south County Dublin.

The second piece is an eighth-century narrative from the Book of Armagh. This concerns the shadowy fifth century bishop Iserninus, one

---

25 Stokes 1890, 239; *CSH* 212, 707.885; O'Keeffe, 21; Ó Riain 1977, 79; Plummer, 7. **26** Ó Raithbheartaigh, 139.

of Patrick's companions, and relates how he was of the Cattraige of Cliu, where he founded several churches. From the context of this piece it is clear that the Cliu meant here is not Cliu in Munster but the Cliu which corresponds to the later territory of Idrone in Co. Carlow. While two of the churches founded here by Iserninus have been tentatively identified there is something quite suspect about this narrative. The juxtaposition of Cattraige and Cliu is one thing, but when we add one of the (unidentified) churches said to have been founded by Iserninus, Láthrach Da *Arad*, we find a third element, Arad – admittedly in a locative rather than ethnic context – reminiscent of Ára Cliach in Munster. Is it simply coincidence that a thirteenth-century church in Ára Cliach was called Latheragh, the modern Laraghlawe? It may be that the eighth century scribe reworked or conflated earlier materials which may have linked Iserninus with Ára Cliach and the Cattraige of that area, perhaps through an incomplete understanding of the import of the material.[27] Whatever of the second piece adduced above, the first reference is unambiguous in locating a branch of the Cattraige in the general area which also included Killiney. Such a sharing of cults between related segments of peoples, some of whom, at least, may have been, like the Cattraige, itinerant ecclesiastical lineages, is well attested and a second tentative example may be proposed from the same region, that of the Uí Liatháin saints mentioned above, the presence of whose cults in Leinster may be attributable to the similar presence of that of a segment of the same people, the Cenél Dalláin, in Laigin Tuathgabair.[28]

If a dedication to his sisters existed in Leinster, why not one to the saint himself? Ó Riain has drawn attention to the common phenomenon of doublets in the early Irish calendars of saints or martyrologies, several causes of which are suggested.[29] While such can occur on different days in the calendar the frequent occurrence of doublets on the same date is germane to the present point. Ó Riain is perhaps best known for his work on the phenomenon of cult fragmentation where he has sought

27 Bieler, 175–6; Hogan, 61; Sweetman, 279. **28** Mac Shamhráin, 207. **29** Ó Riain 1975, 78–80, 87.

to demonstrate the fragmentation of a single cult into that of several
superficially distinct cults over a period of centuries involving the loss
of identity of the original exemplar. The best know example of his work
in this area relates to the cult of Finbarr of Cork, which, he has attempted
to demonstrate, is merely an early offshoot of the cult of Finnian of
Moville, in Ulster.[30]

Ó Riain's methodology, while not meeting with universal acceptance,[31] has possible relevance to the present study, particularly in light
of the very large number of saints bearing the first name Colmán in the
sources. Indeed, it would appear that this first name is the single most
common saints' name occurring during the early period. Ó Riain is on
record as suggesting that the large number of Colmáin occurring in the
sources may be considerably reduced if many of these are viewed as doublets.[32] Whatever of this in general, there is one such possible doublet
which may disguise the early presence of the cult of Colmán of Cloyne
in Leinster, in an area quite near where the cult of his sisters has already
been noted.

One of the features of doublets, as defined by Ó Riain, is the sharing of the same *natalis* or date of death or burial (saint's day), sometimes
where what is patently the same saint is listed twice, often under variants of his/her name or even under variants or fragmentations of his/her
cult. One of our earliest martyrologies, that of *Óengus,* of early ninth-
century date, includes, in addition to our Colmán, another saint of the
name on the same day (24 November), namely Colmán Duib Cuilinn,
a little known saint who merits brief inclusion in one later *vita* (that of
Colmán of Lann Elo) and whose genealogy does not appear to have survived.[33] The possible connection with Mac Léinín can be found in a later
gloss on *Óengus,* which the editor translates as follows:

> Colmán Duib Cuilinn, i.e. black Colmán from Cuilinn, i.e. a
> mountain which is at Belach Conglais in Leinster. Colmán of the

---

30 See note no. 3 in Chapter One. 31 Ó Corráin 1985a; Etchingham 1999, 172–3. 32 Ó
Riain 1975, 79. 33 Stokes 1905, 247; Heist, 216; *CSH,* 707.104.

ink (*duib*) of Cuilinn in the Renna (*Rendaib*), i.e. from Dún Rechet and from Belach Conglais in Leinster and from other places. Comgall of Bangor went to the house of Colmán Duib Cuilinn's father, who had a barren wife. Then the cleric asks writing ink of the barren wife. It is given (and she tastes it). Thereof Colmán is conceived. Hence he was called Colmán of the ink of Cuilinn.

Cuilinn is the modern Coolinarrig, a high hill above Baltinglass (Belach Conglais), Co. Wicklow, where a church site associated with the saint is shown on nineteenth-century OS maps. This lay within the early general polity which on occasion also included Killiney. I would suggest that, whatever the veracity of the above account, the possible link with Colmán of Cloyne, or evidence of cult fragmentation, if you will, is the writing ink. The *filid* class to which our Colmán belonged was, of course, marked by skill in literacy.

In summary then, it is suggested that the evidence adduced in the present chapter is of itself a strong argument for the existence of Mac Léinín, linking him (and his sisters) as it does with an obscure but clearly once powerful people who disappear early from the stage of history. Such early evidence of cult diffusion – with only limited accompanying fragmentation – is a very strong argument, when viewed in tandem with other evidence to be adduced below, for the existence of Léinín and of his children.

CHAPTER FOUR

The king and the saint

4.1 Colmán in the tale of Conall Corc

Our second substantial early reference to the saint comes from another early historico-literary text, *Conall Corc and the Corco Luigde*.[1] This has been identified as a propaganda tract designed to validate the superior claims of the Síl Cathail (the early name of the later Eóganacht Glennamnach) segment of the Eóganachta to the kingship of Munster and has been dated to the reign of their most powerful king, Cathal mac Finguine (721–42).[2] This text contains a number of incidental references to Colmán mac Léinín.

> *Ar it he tri haithlaich Erenn .i. Énna Áirne, Colmán mac Lénéni 7 Mochammóc Inse Celtra. Cethramad athlaech epscop Erc hi Slane Maige Breg. Maleditione Colmán mac Lénéni muri ciuitatis Ressad ceciderunt.*[3]

> For these are the three ex-laymen of Ireland: Énna of Aran, Colmán mac Lénéni and Mochammóc of Inis Celtra. The fourth ex-laymen was bishop Erc in Sláne of Mag Breg. Through the curse of Colmán mac Lénéni the walls of the city of Ressad fell.

> *Siad maic Fiachnai: Oncind; Marcán; Suibne; Maeldúin la Dal Cuirind hi Feic, Sropán; Máel hUmai; Forind la Marthinu. Máel hUmai gabais laim Cholmáin meic Lénéni a Maethalaig 7 hac causa cum fratribus priuatar regno.*[4]

---

1 For the original see Meyer 1910. A translation was published by Hull 1947 and later partly emended by Hull 1958. **2** Byrne 1994, 48; Bhreathnach 1996, 72, 86–7. **3** Meyer 1910, 60. **4** Ibid., 62.

These are the sons of Fiachnae: Oncind; Marcán; Suibne; Máel Dúin [who lives] with Dál Cuirind at Fíac; Srophán; Máel Umai; and Forind [who lives] with the Marthini. Máel Umai expelled Colmán mac Léinín from Maethalach and on that account he and his brothers are deprived of rule.

Coirpri mac Crimthain do-bert Cluain hUama do Dia 7 do Cholman mac Colcen qui et Mac Lénéni 7 Aired Cechtraige 7 Cell Naile. Inde regnum mundi meruerunt.[5]

Coirpre mac Crimthainn it was who gave Cluain Uamha to God and to Colmán mac Colcon[6] who is also called Mac Léinín and Aired Cechtraige and Cell Náile. Because of this they are entitled to secular rule.

The first fragment contains a piece of wisdom literature in the genre of the later triads. Here Colmán is listed among the three ex-laymen of Ireland. The term used here, *athláech*, is to be understood in the present context primarily in the sense of 'ex-layman', one who has entered holy orders in adult life as a 'late vocation', and carries the additional implication of one duly abandoning an important secular career of some kind. (Its literal meaning is 'former warrior', which of itself provides an insight into contemporary society.) There may also be overtones here of adult conversion to Christianity, bearing in mind that Ireland was still only partly evangelized in the sixth century. I will return to this point below (5.3).

The meaning in a political sense of the reference to the walls of Ressad falling as a result of Colmán's curse will be explored below. Suffice it for now to note the phenomenon of the power of a saint's curse as a common theme in Irish hagiography, to which, again, we will return below. The Coirpre mac Crimthainn mentioned in the text was a king of Munster whose obituary is recorded in the annals *sub anno* 580.[7] The

---

5 Ibid. **6** It is interesting that the name Colga also occurs in the later pedigree of Mac Léinín in *CSH* (215.1), five generations above the saint. These references suggest that it may have been the genuine patronym born by Colmán's family, such as *Moccu Colgain. **7** *AI* 580; *AU* 579 (= 580); *A Tig* 579.

lands he gave to Mac Léinín can be identified with Cloyne in Co. Cork
and Erry and Killenaule in Tipperary, both parishes lying some few miles
east of Cashel. The *Conall Corc* text provides a comprehensive early
genealogy of Coirpre's family, beginning with his father, Crimthann
Srem, and this identifies the Máel Umai of the text as nephew to king
Coirpre, the son of his brother Fiachna.[8] Maethalach, from which Máel
Umai drove Mac Léinín, cannot be identified with certainty. These references to Mac Léinín have the strongest whiff of authenticity for several reasons, which will be elaborated below.

4.2 The political background: the Síl Cathail dynasts

To place these references to our subject in context it is first necessary to
describe the political background of the period. The following scenario
has the most support amongst scholars. [9] As the historical curtain lifts
during the sixth century Munster is in turmoil, with its recently established Eóganacht overlords still not firmly established as the fissiparous
remnants of its probable former ruling dynasty, the Dáirine, are driven
to the periphery of the province. In reality the Eóganacht are not a uni-
fied dynasty but a group of politically if not genealogically related and
partly competing lineages. The earliest name of this people, one soon to
become obsolete, is the Uí Meic Láire, and it may well be that Mac Láire
alias Corc was an historical personage, living perhaps in the mid-fifth
century, as he is the apical figure for all true segments of the Eóganacht.
Certainly the earliest traditions regarding this people, which are relatively full, all point clearly in this direction, although it is also possible
that this schema is merely a later construct. It has been suggested that
the Eóganacht originated in west Munster, in what is today Co. Kerry,
and extended their power eastwards into the richer lands of the Golden
Vale. The situation which emerges into the dim light of the proto-his-

---

8 Meyer 1910, 61–2. **9** Ó Buachalla 1952, 1956, passim; Ó Corráin 1972, 1–9; 1985c, 79–80;
Byrne 1973, 207; Ó Coileáin, 43–5.

---

torical period, and which continues for some centuries afterwards, sees a division of Munster into an eastern and western section, Aurmuma and Iarmuma. The eastern section is ruled from Cashel, apparently recently conquered, while the western section is ruled by the Eóganacht of Loch Léin (Killarney), subject only to a loose and contested hegemony from Cashel. The border between both moieties, which will remain constant for over two centuries, runs approximately between the location of the modern cities of Cork and Limerick.

The situation which pertained in the proto-historical period (AD 550–600) was one of near continuous civil war between both halves of Munster. The later historico-literary tales reflect the belief that this situation had prevailed for some time before this and the situation was to prevail until around AD 800. The first king of Cashel about whom some historical certainty exists was Coirpre mac Crimthainn *alias* Coirpre Crom whose annalistic obit of 580 is generally regarded as authentic and who, in one early source, is said to have reigned for 17 years.[10] His relevance to the present study should be obvious. The only other significant annalistic reference to him, as victor at the battle of Femen in 572/3, is probably an erroneous reference to a battle in Meath with which Coirpre had no connexion.[11]

There is sufficient evidence to securely place Coirpre in both his geographical and political context. The genealogies – though not the earliest – bequeath to Coirpre's father, Crimthann, the epithet 'Femin'.[12] This refers to Mag Femin, the plain which lies south of Cashel towards Cahir and which may originally have referred to the area stretching as far east as the slopes of Slievenamon (Sliab ar (or al) Femun) and south to the Suir.[13] By the twelfth century, however, if indeed Mag Femin is identical with the Anglo-Norman cantred of Moyenen, the toponym referred only to the western section of the plain.[14] The familial connexion with Femen is confirmed by the genealogical details of the Síl Cathail contained in *Conall Corc* and the *Corco Luigde*. While several placenames in this early text are now obsolete, we note that the descendants of two

---

10 *A Tig* 578. **11** *AI* 573; *AFM* 571; Ó Corráin 1971. **12** *CGH* 208. **13** Hogan, 408–9, 608. **14** Empey 1970, 27.

of Coirpre's sons are located in Femen at the time of its composition: Cenél Suibni Cailich 'in Femen', descended from Diarmait Find, and the descendants of Forind, grandson of Coirpre, 'who lives with the Marthini', a reference to be understood in the context of that branch of the Martine who lived in Airthir Femin.[15] Furthermore, the church where Coirpre was buried, Cill Cromglais, may also have been in Femen and in one early annal Coirpre was said to have been 'fostered at Cromglais'.[16] (But see below, 6.1). From all of this it seems clear that Coirpre, if not his father, maintained his chief base in Femen, just south and east of Cashel. *Conall Corc* and a number of other early sources suggest that the political situation inherited by Coirpre was one where the eastern Eóganachta had just overthrown the dominance of Daui Iarlaithi, king of Eóganacht Locha Léin and Iarmuma, who seems to have been the most powerful king in Munster. These traditions indicate the involvement of the Uaithne, Fir Maige and Uí Liatháin in the fight against Daui, all peoples living just east of the border between the two Munsters. Furthermore, there is evidence that Coirpre was involved in at least one battle – that of Cluas Óla – with either the son or grandsons of Daui which appears to have resulted in a victory for Coirpre.[17]

4.3 Colmán: patron of Síl Cathail

This, then, is the context in which we must view the references to Coirpre and Mac Léinín. Of the churches said to have been given by the king to the saint Erry and Killenaule, lying four and ten miles respectively east-north-east of Cashel, certainly lay within the eleventh century polity of Eóganacht Chaisil and most likely also did in the sixth century (*A Tig* 1063). Cloyne is much more intriguing. This lay in the territory of Uí Liatháin, a people treated with much respect by later genealogists to the extent of their being given a false Eóganacht connexion, thus disguising their probable Dáirine origin. While this people

---

15 Meyer 1910, 62; Hogan, 535. **16** Hogan, 185; *A Tig* 572/3. **17** Meyer 1910, 61; Ó Buachalla 1954, 118–20.

lay firmly within the Aurmuma sphere their lands were bordered to the west by Iarmuma. Is the gift of Cloyne to Mac Léinín to be seen in light of the common phenomenon of later centuries where recently conquered sword-land on a disputed border is given to the church to deny the possibility of reconquest? Whatever of this the Cloyne estate was large and consisted of land in the heart of the Uí Meic Caille segment of Uí Liatháin, some of the best land in the entire polity.

We come then to Mac Léinín's Jericho-like curse outside the walls of Ressad, with the implication that 'the walls came atumblin down'. An annal of 980 records the death of Donnubán, *rígh Ressad*. This was Donnubán, king of the eastern segment of the Uí Fidgente, the Uí Chairpre, and in his lifetime the most powerful king of the territory which later became Co. Limerick. A second reference to this place occurs in the slightly later Dalcassian propaganda tract, *Cogadh Gaedhel re Gallaibh*, which again suggests usage in the sense of an alternative or archaic name for Uí Chairpre.[18] It would seem, then, that in Mac Léinín's time Ressad was an early stronghold of the Uí Fidgente, located in the eastern part of that kingdom, somewhere in what later became Uí Chairpre. This territory survived as a petty kingdom or local polity in truncated form until the arrival of the Anglo-Normans and its outline was preserved by them in the cantred of Ocarbry. [19] This was essentially the area between Kilmallock and Croom – but including neither – and, as the heartland of the earlier and fuller Uí Chairpre, is the most likely area for the location of Ressad. So much for the location, but what of the context? The Uí Fidgente were an important component people of Iarmuma whose territory lay on the very border with Aurmuma, on the frontline, as it were. The eighth-century prose account of their earlier conflict with the Corcu Óche, elsewhere given an annalistic date of 552/3, firmly identifies them as enemies of the kings of Cashel.[20] We would seem to have here, then, evidence of Mac Léinín acting as intercessor with the divine on behalf of his patrons, the kings of Cashel, against their enemies.

---

18 *AI* 980.2; Todd 1867, 73. **19** Mac Cotter 2000, 61–2. **20** Ó Buachalla 1954, 114–15.

Finally we come to the expulsion of Mac Léinín from Maethalach by Máel Umai. This place cannot now be identified but, given the general context of the references to the various branches of the Síl Cathail in the *Conall Corc* tract, it is not unreasonable to assume that it lay somewhere in the hinterland of Cashel or, at the very least, in the general south Tipperary – south east Limerick area. We have seen how Mac Léinín was patronized by king Coirpre of Cashel, whom he was remembered as repaying by ensuring victory over his enemies, and it seems unlikely that this expulsion would have been countenanced by the king if he were still alive. Given that Máel Umai was Coirpre's nephew it may be that this event took place after the king's death. As we shall see by the suggested chronology of Mac Léinín given below, it would appear that he outlived Coirpre by some years. It is remarkable how forcibly the role of Mac Léinín as legitimizer of the royal status of Síl Cathail is expressed in *Conall Corc*. The legitimacy and right to rule of no less a personage than Cathal mac Finguine, probably the most powerful king in Ireland in his day, is imputed to be a direct result of his ancestor's patronage of Mac Léinín, just as the no doubt miserable status of the discard segment descended from Máel Umai is similarly imputed to the latter's treatment of the man of God. These passages illustrate clearly that the role of Mac Léinín as 'patron saint' of Síl Cathail was already well established by the early eighth century and probably originated with an actual symbiotic relationship between king and monk in the late sixth century. As we shall see below, the mutual dependency between saint (or his cult) and lineage would continue for several centuries after this.

It may be of some relevance to note here the occurrence of what has been described as the 'loathly-lady theme' in early Irish literature.[21] In essence this theme ascribes the success of one segment of a royal lineage over the others as a direct result of the different treatment given to a mythological female figure with overtones of a pagan deity by all segments. In the *Conall Corc* tale the mythical female figure is replaced by our saint. The similarity of this theme to that occurring in *Conall Corc*

---

21 Ó Coileáin, 36–7.

may be just coincidental. The latter reference, of course, may simply be a device to justify the relegation of a discard segment. As we have noted, *Conall Corc* is of early date and seems to be describing events in turn datable to four or five generations before its date of composition. In such a literate society[22] this relatively short time span has few negative implications for the transmission of historical realities, however packaged, and I suspect that the Máel Umai reference may in fact have some historical basis.

22 Ó Corráin 1998.

CHAPTER FIVE

Colmán: *fili* and *athláech*

From what has been adduced above it will be seen that Mac Léinín was
already a person of some notoriety in the late seventh-century while his
cult and connexion with Munster's leading dynasty was already well
established by early in the following century. Two additional sources of
evidence survive which further contribute to our knowledge of the saint.
These are the annals and the fragments of early poetry attributed to Mac
Léinín.

5.1 Colmán in the annals

The Annals of Inisfallen record Mac Léinín's birth *sub anno* 530. The
Annals of Tigernach record his death *sub anno* 598 while *Chronicon
Scotorum* records the event six years later, in 604. The much later composition, the Annals of the Four Masters, places Mac Léinín's death in
600. Of course these are not actual contemporary records but probably
do reflect contemporary record in the archetype of the Irish annals. Their
value lies in their composition by monks probably in possession of materials now lost to us.

5.2 Colmán as fili

We must now turn to the poetry attributed to Mac Léinín. This con-
sists in all of portions of seven distinct poems, and a modern translation
of the entire corpus is given in Appendix C. This 'canon' was delimited
by Thurneysen and Ó Corráin and does not include all poetry attributed to Mac Léinín in the sources, only that which can be shown to be

linguistically datable to the very earliest stratum of written Irish, generally attributed in date to the later sixth or early seventh centuries, and
some of which, along with its attribution, was certainly common knowledge among *literati* in the tenth-century as evidenced by *Cormac's
Glossary*. This poetry has received further attention from Carney and
Henry and its survival appears to be due to its use as teaching material
by the poetry schools, and may thus offer a valuable secondary source
of information on the saint by virtue of its descent *via* the independent
literary milieu (if however, such actually existed in this period, for which
see below).[1] As these compositions attributed to Colmán stand at the
very beginning of Irish vernacular literature we may perhaps think of
our saint as being among the fathers of Irish literature.

The fragments divide into eight verses, two of which appear to
belong to the same poem. Five of the poems deal entirely with secular
matters while the remaining two are religious in nature. Do these fragments contain anything which might help us in our quest? Fragment I
deals with the generosity of a king, Domnall, who apparently gifted the
poet a sword. The ubiquitous nature of this early Irish christian name
must render entirely futile those speculations on a possible identification of this king. Fragment II mentions a place, Dún maic Daim, which
may be associated with a son of Fedelmid Daim Dasachtaich who occurs
in the genealogies in a sixth or seventh century context. His lineage is
the Fir Tamnaich segment of Uí Fidgente of Co. Limerick, a region to
which, as we have seen, Colmán is linked.[2] Fragments IIIa and IIIb mention another king, Fergus, identified in several early glosses with Fergus
Tuile son of Feradach Dornmár of Uí Liatháin. The son of Fergus,
Diucaill, died in 632 – and this would make Fergus an exact contemporary of Colmán, and very possibly king of Uí Liatháin in his time.[3]
IIIb mentions the chariots of the poets entertained by Fergus, once again
emphasizing the great antiquity of the material to hand. IV is by far the
most interesting of the fragments. This is thought to derive from a eulogy
upon the death of the king mentioned therein, Áed Sláne, an important

1 Stokes 1868, 10, 42; Carney, 63–5; Henry, 146, 214–16. **2** *CGH* p. 233. **3** *CS* 632; *AFM* 627;
CGH p. 224.

king of the Southern Uí Néill in Meath. Áed's murder is recorded in the annals *sub anno* 604,[4] thus again agreeing with the chronology of the annals in relation to Mac Léinín. The remaining verses, V and VI, are religious in nature, the former concerning a vision the poet experienced of heaven, earth and hell during Lent, and the latter mentioning the Apostle Peter.

Fragment IV suggests that even after becoming a monk the poet continued to practise his art. This raises the question of the authenticity of the attribution of these poems to Mac Léinín. Clearly any certainty in this matter is beyond the power of the modern historian to achieve, but even allowing for the possibility that not all of these fragments are correctly attributed, the very ancient and consistent tradition that Mac Léinín was their author is of itself a very powerful argument in favour of the position that our saint was indeed a very famous poet in his time. It will be seen therefore that the chronology of Mac Léinín as first indicated in the *Conall Corc* tale, and subsequently reflected in annalistic computation, is once again confirmed in the poetry. When taken together, the references to the saint in *Conall Corc* and the poetry attributed to Mac Léinín make a very strong argument for acceptance of the essence of the cult of Saint Colmán as reflecting the real life of an early Irish *fili* and ecclesiastic.

5.3 *Colmán as* athláech

Further early evidence for the poetical vocation of our subject may be found in the use of the term *athláech* to describe Colmán in *Conall Corc*, as quoted above. While this may simply and correctly be translated as 'ex-layman' the term has much wider implications germane to the present study. The vernacular term *láech* and its Latin equivalent, *laicus*, have been the subject of recent research and comment and, as is normal for the period under discussion, complete agreement concerning the

4 *AU* 603 (= 604); *CS* 604.

meaning of the term does not exist among period-scholars.⁵ Sharpe recognized that both terms carry the basic meaning 'layman' and the extended meaning 'warrior', and went on to associate further connotations of 'brigand' and even 'pagan' with the term. The meaning 'brigand' for *láech* seems quite admissible here given its occurrence in the early literature to refer to members of juvenile or young-adult warrior-bands or outlaw groups operating on the fringes of society (*díbergaig* or *fianna*) but Etchingham rejects Sharpe's further connotation of paganism as not warranted by the evidence. It would seem safe then to allow that the term *láech* can be understood in a general way as an inclusive term for various classes of laypersons whose activities put them at odds with the moral programme of the early Christian Church in Ireland, or, as Etchingham puts it, 'it [*laicus*] often seems to denote, rather, grievously sinful laity, of whom a commitment to repentance and emendment is required'. This comment should be understood against the general background as outlined by Etchingham and others of an early Irish Church comprised of a dominant clerical elite and a subservient para-monastic laity (*manaig*) who together seem to comprise a numerical minority within society, the majority being viewed distastefully by the Church as merely nominal and apparently non-practicing Christians.

I would suggest that it is – on one level – in this general context that Colmán is referred to in *Conall Corc*, that of one once 'of the world' with all its sinful connotations and now 'of the church'. Given, therefore, that *laicus* is used as a collective term for various worldly (and anti-Christian?) occupations, which of these is applicable to Colmán? The more extreme among such occupations or transgressions are listed in several early (seventh and eighth century) ecclesiastical sources and one such list includes a *magus* 'wizard, druid', a *díbergach* 'warrior gang member' pledged to evil, an adulterer or one guilty of illegitimate sexual behaviour, a satirist (*praeco*) and a heretic, while another includes killers, thieves, adulterers, perjurers, *magi*, and *praecones* 'satirists'. Yet another brief list mentions disparagingly the druid, *díbergach* and satirist (*cáinte*). The occurrence

---

5 Etchingham 1999, 290–318; Sharpe 1979, 77–9, 88–90.

of the satirist or *cáinte* among these sinful and strongly disapproved of occupations is of interest.[6]

The nature of pre-Christian Celtic Irish society is – and is likely to remain permanently – the object of more speculation than certainty, primarily due to the lack of evidence for this society which may be principally attributed to the early Irish Church's virtual monopoly of contemporary historiography. It is generally agreed that the various grades of poet, ranging from learned and literate *filid* at the top of the scale, through the illiterate or orally based *baird* below them down to the various lesser groups on the fringes or even outside of lawful society, of which the term *cáinti* may be a collective, inherited some of the features of the pagan Celtic *veleta*. These principally included the powers of eulogy and its obverse, satire, but also carry overtones of druidic or shamanistic functions, such as dealer in magic, weaver of spells or incantations, and seer or prophet. The role of the low-grade and illiterate *cáinti* has been defined as 'the use of satire for gain rather than for its properly defensive use to avenge wrongdoing', and this category of poet is associated with *díbergaig* groups and the use of satire for wrongful or unlawful gain.[7]

It is unlikely that the term *athláech* as applied to Mac Léinín is to be understood in this sense as it would appear that he may already have been a member of the *filid* class before his 'elevation' from the secular to the clerical, and it is probably to his membership of this latter profession that the designation *athláech* pertains. This brings us to another problem, for virtually nothing is known about this class in Mac Léinín's period. Indeed it has been suggested that this group early made common cause with the new Christian creed in opposition to the druids and lesser grades of satirists who maintained opposition to the new religion for a period after its arrival.[8] More intriguingly, it has been suggested that, at least in the period after 700, the art of *filidecht*, or, more specifically, its teaching, was confined to the monasteries, most of which maintained

---

6 Etchingham 1999, 302–3, 316. 7 Bergin, 4; Caerwyn-Williams, 31–33; McCone, 221–8. 8 McCone, 22–5.

schools of *filidecht*, each under a (clerical?) professor of the subject, where lay pupils were taught. While this proposition seems to be untestable it would appear that no evidence survives from this period for the existence of secular schools of *filidecht*.[9] A germane issue is the probable linkage between the arrival of Christianity and of writing in Ireland, and by implication the putative Christianity of the literate *filid* class who, at a slightly later period, certainly appear to live clearly within the Christian 'pale', as evidenced by the practice of monogamy among this class in contradistinction to the polygamy of other senior castes in society.[10] If the very ancient written traditions – for they can be described as nothing less – which place Mac Léinín at the font of Gaelic literature in Ireland reflect historical reality, does it not follow that we have here some indication of the existence of a secular school of *filidecht* as early as the mid-sixth century? Unless, of course, he was trained in a monastic school of *filidecht* if such existed at this time? And does it not also follow as a distinct possibility that perhaps Mac Léinín himself founded a clerical school of *filidecht* in Cloyne before 600 AD, a suggestion supported by tentative evidence adduced by Ó Corráin?[11] (The tenth century *Triads* describe Cloyne as an important law school).[12] Before leaving this discussion it may be noted that some confirmation of the view that Mac Léinín was a lay *fili* before taking clerical orders may be found in the triad quoted above listing 'the three *athláich* of Ireland'. One of the others was Énna of Aran, the traditions concerning whom suggest him to have been the heir to a powerful kingdom before surrendering to his clerical vocation. His genealogy seems to confirm this tradition in that it makes him one of the sons of Conall mac Daimíne, an important figure in the early secular Airgialla pedigrees, from whom, *via* various sons, several later branches of this people are derived.[13] This is in marked contrast to the usual saintly pedigree, in which the subject is joined to an important lineage *via* a remote and otherwise unattested – and patently fictitious – line of ancestors. Apparently Colmán's qualification for mem-

---

9 Ibid., 26. **10** Ó Corráin, et al., 1984, 400–4. **11** Ó Corráin 1980, 160–1. **12** Meyer 1906, 2. **13** Todd 1864, 21 March; *CGH* 140, 414.

bership of this triad was his career as a secular *fili* just as Énna's was his status as a princely member of an important lineage.

The incident, referred to earlier, where Colmán cursed Ressad, bringing its walls down, may contain further resonances of his first career. Saintly cursing is a common theme in Irish hagiography, and such examples as those of *Betha Adamnáin*, where the saint curses opponents for affronting his community and curses various kings for taking imposts from monastic lands and for slaying one under the saint's protection, readily spring to mind. Similar examples can be quoted in the case of Patrick, Colmcille and many other saints.[14] In the present case Colmán's curse may have had additional potency in light of his former career as a *fili*. Colmán's curse at Ressad probably took the form such actions are usually depicted as taking in both hagiography and historiography by saint and satirist alike, i.e. of an incantatory verse, and it has been suggested that this form of 'magic' is essentially the same whether practised by saint as curse or by *fili* as *áer* or satire, both representing the older inherited pagan power of the *magus*.[15] The actual Latin wording of the Ressad cursing reference is *maleditione*, from *maledictum* 'curse'. This term was early borrowed into Old Irish to give *malidacht* (later *mallacht*), which can have the specific meaning of a saint's curse, thus implying that Colmán had already embarked on his second, ecclesiastical career when he cursed the walls of Ressad.[16] To stay with the theme of 'magic' and the joint saintly and *fili* inheritance, it has been suggested that both *sanctus* and *fili* also inherited the earlier druidic power of prophecy, and this was certainly the image of Colmán held by the Dalcassian propagandist writing in the eleventh century when describing our saint as *fáidh agus file* 'prophet and poet'.[17]

The putative Christianity of the early and literate *filid* class as noted above implies that Mac Léinín may have been, at least nominally, a Christian before he surrendered to his vocation. Can we find some support for this implication in his name, Colmán, a name of Latin and thus

---

14 Stokes 1887, 203; Herbert 1988b, 50–3; O'Kelleher, 141. **15** Ó Cathasaigh. **16** Ibid.; RIA *Dictionary of the Irish language.* **17** McCone, 228; Todd 1867, 85.

Christian etymology? As against this an early tract on the alias of the saints gives 'Colmán *alias* Mac Lenin', suggesting that perhaps Mac Léinín is to be understood as a first name rather than a patronym, and thus that Colmán may have been a name 'taken in religion'.[18] This however does not agree with the earliest literary references to the saint as adduced in Chapter 3 above, nor with the early traditions concerning his sisters, 'the daughters of Léinín'. The implication here must be that Colmán was his given name and Mac Léinín a patronym used, not unusually, as an alias, and thus that our saint was at least nominally a Christian before his late vocation.

5.4 Colmán in religion

The question now arises, what of the nature of Colmán's spiritual mission? The answer must be, in our present state of knowledge concerning the very early Irish Church, we do not and probably never will know. Currently the nature of the Irish Church even in the later and better documented period after AD 700 is the object of much scholarly debate and disagreement and, if we are to be honest, not much is known of the Church in the sixth century and the fatuous speculations of historians of earlier generations have served merely to muddy the waters. No valid tradition survives to indicate that Colmán held episcopal office and his clerical rank must have been below this. The belief that he was buried in Cloyne, which can be traced, in all probability, to at least the tenth century, lends support to the view implicit in one of the *Conall Corc* references and indeed in those of the glosses on the martyrologies, that Cloyne was his chief foundation and 'place of resurrection'. (See below, 7.1, 7.2). The exact nature of the ecclesiastical community he founded here cannot be known. One should be wary of the automatic assumption that it was 'a monastery' in any modern sense, given that, even in relation to the later period, the exact meaning of this term is only now being elucidated.

---

18 *CSH* 703.15.

5.5 Colmán: a life in summary

Before we move on to the history of his cult here is probably a good place to summarize what may now, in the absence of hyperscepticism, be reasonably inferred about Colmán Mac Léinín. Born to a branch of the Cattraige resident in the hinterland of Emly, he appears to have been raised, at least nominally, as a Christian. Colmán had been educated as a *fili*, a powerful group within society, Christian by association, and thus must have come from a family of some wealth and social status. After a career as a successful *fili*, Colmán answered the calling to a clerical vocation. At some stage, (after his achievement of clerical status?), Colmán formed a relationship with Coirpre mac Crimthainn, king of Munster, which saw the cleric cursing the king's enemies, apparently with some success, and accordingly being rewarded by the king with land in several locations in Munster on which to found ecclesiastical establishments. All of these events must have occurred before Coirpre died, probably around AD 580. After the king's death the cleric somehow became involved in factional strife between Coirpri's descendants in which some of them persecuted the cleric while others, the ancestors of the later dominant line, protected him. Colmán's chief ecclesiastical foundation and probable place of burial was at Cloyne, and he died sometime around AD 600, and where he may have left a school of poetry in existence. The calendars are unanimous in dating his death on 24 November.

CHAPTER SIX

Eóganacht Glennamnach: sponsors
of a cult

Turning to the dynamics of cult development, we note Mac Shamhráin's comment that 'it would seem reasonable to assume that certain dynasties, were, at different stages, predisposed towards the adoption and subsequent promotion of particular saints' cults'.[1] This phenomenon is, in fact, relatively well documented. Several examples of such relationships can be given. Finnian of Clonard and the Uí Maelseachlainn kings of Meath, Brigit of Kildare and the Uí Dúnlainge, Colmcille of Iona and the Cenél Conaill of Ulster and Clann Cholmáin of Meath, the Armagh based Patrician cult and the Cenél Eógain and, much nearer to home, the cult of Finbarr and the Uí Echach Raithlind.[2] I hope to demonstrate presently that to this list can be added that of Colmán Mac Léinín and the Eóganacht Glennamnach and their descendants, the Uí Chaím. The historiography of this dynasty has been hitherto incomplete and marred by the assumption, the result of incomplete research, that the Fermoy district of Co. Cork only became the chief powerbase of the dynasty very late in its life. As we shall see below, this assumption is a serious error. We have seen from what has been adduced above that, as early as *circa* 730, Colmán's cult was an important legitimizing element in the rule of the Síl Cathail, a relationship which would continue for several centuries after this. The evidence suggests that the changing geographical location of Colmán's cult during these centuries is directly related to the changing location of the power-base of this Eóganacht dynasty. In order to explore this relationship fully we must first examine the history of Eóganacht Glennamnach, the full rel-

1 208. 2 Hughes, 18–19; Mac Shamhráin, 133–5; Herbert 1988a, 54, 63–7; Ó Riain 1994, 234 note 11, 250 note 173.

evance of which to the cult of Colmán will only emerge in the later chapters of this work.

6.1 The Síl Cathail segment of Eóganacht Chaisil

The term Glennamnach probably derives from Gleanndomain, a toponym from which the modern Glanworth, a town a few miles north-west of Fermoy, is the present English form.[2a] Gleanndomain itself was a demesne or mensal *tuath* of this dynasty, originally one of several, but which had become the main base of the dynasty by the mid-eighth century at the latest. In the eighth century this dynasty were referred to as Cenél or Síl Cathail, the probable eponym being Cathal mac Aeda Flainn Cathrach, king of Cashel in the 620s. This Cathal was the grandson of Coirpre mac Crimthainn, Mac Léinín's benefactor.

I have already (4.2) discussed the origins of the principal Eóganacht dynasties who first came to prominence in the historical period in the person of Coirpre Crom or mac Crimthainn (*obit* 580). The Eóganacht pedigree, for what it is worth, derives the later lines of the then dominant Eóganacht Chaisil from Fedelmid, son of Óengus mac Nad Fraich (*obit* 490), and their nearest relatives, Eóganacht Glennamnach and Eóganacht Airthir Chliach, from another son of Óengus, Eochu (grandfather of Coirpre Crom).[3] The remaining Eóganacht lines are shown as earlier or more distant offshoots of this main stem. The nomenclature used in this schema is that of the tenth century, reflecting the dominance of the various lines claiming descent from Fedelmid at the expense of what had by then become regnal discard segments. A close study of the sources reveals a very different picture from that presented by this nomenclature. In the earlier period the kingship passed between several distinct Eóganacht groups, none dominating to the exclusion of the others. The strongest dynasty in this period was Síl Cathail. While the various king lists and

2a Kenneth Nicholls, however, suggests an alternative derivation from Gleann *Odhar or *Omhair which would account for the early forms Glennoure, Glennowyr, etc. **3** *CGH* 195–7.

annals invariably do not fully agree it is possible to get a reasonably clear picture on the descent of the kingship of Munster in this period.[4] Between 580 and 821 at least seven and perhaps as many as nine members of Síl Cathail held the kingship. This compares with just five kings for their nearest rivals, the several distinct lines of descendants of Fedelmid who may be described under the later umbrella term, Eóganacht Chaisil. Thus in a period in which approximately twenty kings reigned, more than one third of these were members of Síl Cathail. This picture is reflected in the earliest substantial Eóganacht pedigrees, which can in part be dated to the mid-eighth century. In these the senior line of Eóganacht Chaisil, given pride of place before all of the others, are none other than Síl Cathail in a pedigree which ends with the great king, Cathal mac Finguine (721–42).[5] Cathal thus considered himself to be the most senior among the Eóganacht Chaisil nobles and it would appear that the genealogical separation of Síl Cathail from Eóganacht Chaisil only occurred after the former lost out finally to the descendants of Fedelmid in the competition for the kingship of Cashel in the mid-ninth century.

We have already seen how Coirpre Crom appeared to have had his chief power-base around Femen, south of Cashel. We have also noted the existence of junior branches of Síl Cathail here in the eighth century but by the eleventh century it is clear that the then kingdom of Eóganacht Chaisil, whose bounds did not extend west of Cashel itself to any great extent but lay chiefly to north and east of it, was primarily the preserve of the descendants of Fedelmid.[6] The evidence concerning Síl Cathail demonstrates that its powerbase had, apparently during the seventh century if not even earlier, shifted westwards and southwards to the border or marchlands with Iarmuma. It seems a reasonable conclusion to attribute this movement to the pivotal role played by Síl Cathail in the eternal if intermittent war with Iarmuma, known from the sources to have raged between both moieties of Munster from the very dawn of proto-history until the early ninth century.[7]

---

4 For a useful summary of the information see Byrne's pedigree in *A new history of Ireland*, ix, 136. Sources for the king-lists are listed in Ní Dhonnchadha, 198 note 2. 5 *CGH* 197–8. 6 Hogan, 399; *A Tig* 1063; Empey 1970, 27. 7 Ó Buachalla 1952, 77–81; 1954, 118–21.

After the death of Coirpre Crom his son, Fedelmid, may have held the kingship of Cashel for some years after 583. After some decades in which the kingship was held by various branches of Eóganacht, includ-ing, significantly, Áed Bennán of Eóganacht Locha Léin (and thus also king of Iarmuma), Coirpre's grandson, Cathal mac Áeda, regained the throne, which he held probably between 619 to 628. After him ruled two descendants of Fedelmid mac Óengusa interspersed with one king of Eóganacht Áine before Síl Cathail regained power in 662. In this period, however, the annals give prominence to Óengus Liath, younger brother of Cathal who died in 628 and obviously head of Síl Cathail, although he is nowhere referred to as king of Cashel. Under annals of 640, 643 and 645,[8] is recorded the battle of Cathair Cinn Con between Óengus Liath 'from Áine' and Mael Dúin, king of Iarmuma. One entry says that there was much slaughter on both sides while another states that Mael Dúin fled. Cathair Cinn Con is now Rockbarton, near Bruff, in Co. Limerick, which lies on the erstwhile border between Iarmuma and Aurmuma in the same general area as Ressad, where earlier Colmán and his patron, Coirpre Crom were apparently active against Iarmuma. Under entries for 642 and 646 are recorded the death of Óengus Liath.[9] While these are jumbled, the most reliable is likely to be that from the local Annals of Inisfallen, which record the death 'of Óengus Liath from Áine at Glennamain'. Some of the other entries simply describe Óengus as 'of Glind Damáin'. While these references to Gleanndomain are the first certain association of Síl Cathail with this place it is possible if not indeed probable that the Cill Cromglais where Coirpre Crom was said to have been fostered and later buried (4.2) did not in fact lie in Femen at all but is to be identified with the place of that name, now obsolete, which lay just south of Glanworth as indicated in the topographical tract, *Crichad an Chaoille*.[10] If this were so it would link the Gleanndomain

8 *CS* 639 (=640); *AU* 639 (= 640), 642 (= 643); *A Tig* 640; *AI* 645. For Óengus Liath's place in the Síl Cathail pedigree see Ó Donnchadha, 144. **9** *A Tig, AU* 641 (=642); *AI* 646. **10** Power 1932, 46. The statement that Coirpre was buried in Cill Cromglais is found in *Conall Corc* and is thus early. The earliest attribution placing this church in Femen appears to be from the twelfth century *Cóir Anmann* and may simply be a mistake. A rectory of 'Kylcromglassy' survived into the sixteenth century located near Glanworth, but its exact

estate with Síl Cathail since the late sixth century. This probability merits serious consideration if we accept that the same Coirpre endowed Mac Léinín with Cloyne. The references to Áine (now Knockainy near Hospital), indicate that Síl Cathail must have possessed additional mensal lands north of Gleanndomain, in what is today south eastern Limerick.

The next Síl Cathail king of Cashel was Cathal *alias* Cú Cen Mathair, son of king Cathal, who reigned between 662 and 666. A reference to him in *Conall Corc* indicates that he was overlord of the Corcu Bascind in western Clare and thus undisputed lord of both Munsters.[11] It would appear that between 678 and around 700 two sons of Cú Cen Mathair, Ailill and Finguine, successively held the kingship, Ailill until about 695 and Finguine after. Ailill is described as *Rí Muigi Féne* (king of Fir Maige) in the guarantor list of Cáin Adomnáin.[12] While the list itself has been shown to be contemporary with the promulgation (made in 697) the titles attached to the guarantors are the work of a later scribe, not datable with certainty but certainly to within at most two generations of 697.[13] It is probable that Ailill was in fact king of Cashel in 697. Implicit in the title given to Ailill during the first half of the eighth century is the position of Gleanndomain as by then the principal base of this royal lineage.

Finguine was the father of Cathal mac Finguine, king of Munster between 721 and 742, and probably the most powerful king of Munster yet to have reigned. In addition to being undisputed king of the province Cathal established some level of lordship over Leinster and even harried the southern Uí Néill lands in Meath, exploits which resulted in his becoming a saga king in the literature. Upon his death, in 742, he was buried in the monastery of Emly and the local annalists describe him,

location is, unfortunately, now lost. (Hull 1947, 904; Stokes 1895b, 310; *PRIA* 35 C, p. 161). **11** Meyer 1910, 60. **12** Meyer 1905, 19. **13** Ní Dhonnchadha 214–15. Ní Dhonnchadha appears to have based her opinion that the titles attached to the guarantor list were added at various times, some centuries later, on the title *Rí Muigi Féne* as attached to Ailill, as she believed that 'Eóganacht Glennamnach did not occupy Fir Maige Féne until centuries after his [Ailill's] death' (201). In light of the revised position proposed in the present work for the arrival of Síl Cathail in Fir Maige I would suggest a much earlier dating for the titles than that proposed by Ní Dhonnchadha as the only 'late' evidence adduced by her, that concerning Ailill, has now been shown to be erroneous.

with perhaps justifiable hyperbole, as *Rí hÉrend*.[14] A eulogy written upon his death describes his Gleanndomain estate as mensal (*Seacht mbali Cathail cen cháin*) but goes on to make special play of describing him as king of both Déisi and Áine, once again indicating that his paternal estate extended north from Glanworth towards Áine and Déis Becc.[15] Cathal's death ushered in a long period of Iarmuma dominance in the person of Mael Dúin of Eóganacht Locha Léin, who ruled as king of Munster between 742 and his death in 786, although not without opposition from Aurmuma. After this service was resumed as usual with the accession of Artríg, son of Cathail mac Finguine, probably the first king of Munster to be anointed in the modern Christian fashion, in 793.[16] Artríg was also innovative in his proclamation of the Law of Ailbe at Emly, thus keeping Munster in step with legal advances occurring elsewhere in Ireland.[17] While Artríg's death is recorded in 821 it is certain that he had resigned the kingship some years before, probably in favour of his son, Tuathal, who appears to have died *in vita patris*. The deaths of father and son brought to an end the centuries of Síl Cathail dominance of the kingship of Munster. When the death of Donnubán, another son of Artríg, occurs in 831 he is simply styled *rí Glennamnach*.[18] One final effort to regain power may have been made by the shadowy figure of Finguine, grandson – or more likely, great-grandson – of Artríg, mentioned in just one regnal list,[19] who appears to have flourished late in the ninth century and who, if he did indeed succeed to the throne of Cashel, must have held it 'with opposition' and certainly not for long.

An interesting and apparently hitherto unnoticed facet of the centuries of conflict between Iarmuma and Aurmuma was the pattern of marriage allliance between leading dynasties as revealed in the few early Munster marriage records contained in the source known as the *Banshenchas*. Here marriages strictly followed the divide between east and west, with Eóganacht Locha Léin, Eóganacht Raithlind and Uí

---

14 *AI* 721, 735, 742; *A Tig* 720, 734, 736, 737, 741; *AU* 720, 732, 736; *AFM* 717, 731, 734. For an account of Cathal see Ó Riain 1978, xii–xv. **15** Best and O'Brien, 19165–19215. **16** *A Clon* 790; *AU* 792 (= 793). **17** Etchingham 1999, 194–209. **18** *AI* 831. **19** Ó Donnchadha 405.

Fidgente intermarrying on the one side while Eóganacht Chaisil, Déisi and Uí Liatháin similarly related on the other. One additional early link between Síl Cathail and the Cloyne area is suggested by the marriage of Cathal mac Finguine to Cailleach, daughter of Dunchad mac Ronáin, king of Uí Liatháin (and therefore sister of Anmchad, eponym of the later regnal family of Uí Anmchada).[20]

The disappearance of Síl Cathail from the exercise of power in Munster and their transformation from first among Eóganacht Chaisil to being outsiders under a new dynastic name, Eóganacht Glennamnach, are developments remarkable for their suddenness. Can we find some reason for these dramatic developments? I believe we can. The dominant politic in early Munster was the competition between east and west Munster, or Eóganacht Locha Léin and the various eastern Eóganachts, in which, as we have seen, Síl Cathail played a prominent part. Indeed the dominant position held by Síl Cathail in Aurmuma must be principally attributed to its position as defender of the marches, given that its territory seems to have lain along an axis from Glendomain to Áine, thus virtually all lying along the border with Iarmuma. It can hardly be coincidental that, just at the very time the power of Síl Cathail was waning, so too, in virtually a local revolution, the long established overlordship of the Eóganacht Locha Léin was overthrown by their Kerry neighbours, the Ciarraige, in an even more dramatic fashion in the first years of the ninth century. With the *ráison d'être* of Síl Cathail dominance gone power shifted eastwards to those dynasties descended from Fedelmid, especially the Cenél Fáilbe Flaind, whose kings would be much concerned with first resisting Uí Néill expansion and later the new north-south orientation in Munster politics represented by the threat of the *arriviste* Dál Cais.

6.2 The northern lands of Síl Cathail

This leads us to a discussion of the location of the northern lands of Síl Cathail, as we have already clearly identified those southern lands of the

20 Dobbs (1930–2), 47/331, 47/333, 48/182, 48/223.

dynasty which lay in what is today Co. Cork. Clearly Síl Cathail were often suzerain over the lesser Eóganacht Áine whose territories lay around and immediately west of the major monastery of Emly, itself an important base for the exercise of power by Síl Cathail on occasion. Where then was the local powerbase of Síl Cathail here? There were a number of lesser Eóganacht territories just west of Eóganacht Chaisil itself, such as Eóganacht Becc, around Donohill, and yet again further west Eóganacht Ua Cathbad around Doon and Solohead on the Limerick/Tipperary border.[21] It is immediately south of Emly that we should look, however, for our answer, to the territory or lordship known to the Anglo-Normans as Natherlach (Aherlow). This was essentially the south-eastern corner of Co. Limerick and the adjacent part of Tipperary: Kilbeheny, Anglesborough, Galbally and Aherlow, the lands wrapped around the western Galtee Mountains.[22] The pre-twelfth-century lordship of this territory is unclear as its later lords, the Meic Briain of Aherlow, descend from Brian Ua Briain slain at Glanmire in 1118, and may have occupied the territory during the course of the first half of the twelfth century. (This is predicated on the assumption that, as was normally the case, the colonial lordship of Natherlach followed the boundaries of a native pre-invasion territory.)[23] As against this dating, it will be noted that, as claimant to the kingship of Munster, Donnchad mac Brian Boraime, grandfather of Brian of Glanmire, maintained a border fortress at Dún Trí Liag in Natherlach in 1054 and the Uí Briain presence here may have continued from this date.[24] The topographical tract, *Crichad an Chaoilli*, shows that the southern part of this territory was still being claimed as part of the Uí Chaím lordship of Fir Maige in the twelfth century.[25] Perhaps more dramatic evidence of Síl Cathail presence from early times in this area is the presence of another Gleanndomain here, which may even be the original toponym and have given its name to the southern

---

21 Eóganacht Becc survived as the Anglo-Norman theudum of Yonachbeg while the eponyms of Eóganacht Ua Cathbad were remembered in the seventeenth-century placenames Tuoghogaffoe and Glennogaffoe in Doon Parish (*Cal. Ormond deeds*, i, 11; *Cal. Irish pat. rolls Jas. I*, 146; *Civil survey*, ii, 11, 75, 78; *Hibernia Delinatio* (map). I am indebted to Mr Kenneth Nicholls for assistance on this point. **22** Empey 1981, 3, 27. **23** See my 'Cantred and Tríucha Céad' (forthcoming). **24** *AFM*. **25** Power 1932, 47–8.

Gleanndomain at Glanworth. Its exact location is unclear. It occurs in *Crichad* and later under the form Glendowan as a fourteenth century knights' fee and chapel, when held of the lords of Natherlach by the Caunteton lords of Fermoy, and appears to be the seventeenth century Glencondon. The actual site of its chapel may be the church site in Kilglass and the super-denomination itself seems to have lain between Mitchelstown and Anglesborough.[26] One further possible connexion between Natherlach and Fermoy is the name of a hill above Kilfinnane, on the western borders of Natherlach, Benyvoughella. The Uí Buachalla occur in *Crichad an Chaoilli* as settled on the banks of the Blackwater.[27] Thus the early mensal lands of Síl Cathail can be shown to have formed an almost continuous line from Emly south to the Blackwater. In light of the political scene in mid eleventh-century Munster as discussed in the following section it would seem reasonable to conclude that Eóganacht Glennamnach began to lose control of these northern lands between Emly and Anglesborough in the face of Uí Briain aggression during the 1050s.

6.3 Eóganacht Glennamnach

Discovering the later history of Síl Cathail, or Eóganacht Glennamnach as they had become by the early ninth century, is greatly hampered by the dearth of annalistic evidence for Desmuma during the tenth and eleventh centuries. Between the obit of Donnubán mac Artríg in 831 and the renewed annalistic coverage of Desmuma in the early twelfth century we have just three annals concerning the dynasty. The Annals of Inisfallen record the death of Gorman mac Mugróin, 'rí Glennamnach', in 891, those of Tigernach record the slaying of the Hua Findgaine 'rí Eoghanachta Glendamnach' in 1046, while *sub anno* 1057 is recorded the slaying of 'Finnguine Ua Finnguine rídomna Muman' at the hands of the king of neighbouring Déisi, Mael Seachlainn Ua Bric.[28]

---

26 See my 'Canted and Tríucha Céad', forthcoming. **27** Power 1932, 49. **28** *AI* 891; *AFM* 1046; *AU*, *ALC*, 1057. The reference from 1046 was misread by the Four Masters who ren-

The annals from 1046 and especially 1057 are very significant. The reference to Finguine Ua Finguine as *rígdamna Muman* can only mean that the family were at this time among the chief players on the political scene in Munster. A survey of the politics of the province around this time presents an interesting picture. The Dál Cais, riven by internal dissensions, had lost control of much of central and southern Munster and were so weak as to be unable to capitalize on a similar division among Eóganacht Chaisil. This polity was divided in two, its eastern section, under its Uí Donnchada kings and their Ossrige allies being unable to overcome the kings of the western section between Emly and Cashel, the ancestors of the later Meic Carthaig kings of Desmuma. The only uniting factor was the mutual loathing of both for the Dál Cais. When we add to this recipe a resurgent Eóganacht Glennamnach under its powerful Uí Finguine kings we must suspect that the hidden strength which protected this western moiety of Eóganacht Chaisil from defeat on the war it was fighting on two fronts was an alliance with Eóganacht Glennamnach to the south, whose kings at this time were challenging for the very kingship of Munster itself.[29] Thus we find at least two periods – around 900 and again in the mid-eleventh century – after their fall from political power in Munster after 821 when Eóganacht Glennamnach again challenge for political lordship in the province. Therefore it is hardly surprising to find their Uí Chaím kings as second in precedence only to the Meic Carthaig kings of Desmuma when a consistent annalistic record resumes in the early twelfth century.

Turning to the Eóganacht genealogies for the period, we find that apart from those of Eóganacht Chaisil the remainder are in poor condition and are either hopelessly confused or missing several generations. The latter situation, of 'lameness', applies to the pedigree of Eóganacht Glennamnach. This ends with the Finguine Ua Caoimh, 'rí Glennamnach', slain in 1135, and lists seven intermediate generations between

---

dered it 'Eóganacht Caill na Manach' thus creating a completely fictitious Eóganacht whose existence has since perplexed historians. **29** For the evidence on which this analysis is based see my forthcoming 'The rise of the Meic Carthaig and the political geography of Desmumu' in *Peritia* 16.

him and king Artríg who died in 821.[30] Based on the customary three
generations per century this pedigree is missing two or three generations.
One of these can be supplied by the annal of 891 adduced above which
suggests that we should insert Mugrón between Artríg and Gorman. The
latter died in 891 and is made father to the Finguine who was making
some claim on the kingship of Munster around 900, which suggests the
genealogy is correct here. The pedigree continues with the eponymous
Caím, father of Cathal, father of Donnchad, father of Aed, father of
Domnall, father of Finguine of 1135. It seems that, as often happened,
rival lines developed claiming the kingship and adopting the surname
of a powerful or memorable ancestor, one descended from the Finguine
of 900, the other from his son (?), Caím, who must also have been king
of Eóganacht Glennamnach. While the Uí Finguine were dominant in
the period 1046–57 power later passed to the Uí Chaím. In the twelfth
century tract, *Crichad an Chaoilli*, these septs still lived in close proximity to each other in Glenndomain (Glanworth).[31]

It is only with the resumption of annalistic evidence after 1100 that
we can begin to assess the condition of the kingdom of Glennamnain.
Annalistic entries concerning Finguine Ua Caoimh (which cover the
period 1121–35) show him to have been one of the leading nobles of the
McCarthy kingdom of Desmuma.[32] This evidence is supplemented in a
most graphic way in the contemporary McCarthy propaganda tract,
Caithréim Cellacháin Chaisil, which, in giving a mostly fictional account
of tenth-century Munster, is thought to mirror policital realities of early
twelfth-century Desmuma. In this tract, Finguine's representative,
Donnchad mac Caím, is described in terms which show him as way and
above the most important of the nobles of Desmuma and virtually *rígdamna* of the kingdom.[33] This situation is further indicated by the placing of the Eóganacht Glennamnach pedigree in second place after that
of the Meic Carthaig themselves in contemporary Eóganacht genealogies.[34] By the early twelfth century, then, the Uí Chaím were one of the

---

30 *CGH* p. 363. **31** Power 1932, 45. **32** *MIA* 1121.2, 1123.2, 1128.2, 1135.2; *AI* 1127.6, 1128.3;
ALC 1135; *AFM* 1135. **33** Bugge, 5, 6, 49; Ó Corráin 1974, 16–18. **34** *CGH* pp. 362–3.

most powerful septs in Desmuma. Lack of evidence makes it difficult to delineate precisely the extent of the sept's local power, which must, however, have been considerable. The topographical tract, *Crichad an Chaoilli*, which seems to date from the period immediately preceding the Anglo-Norman invasion, does offer evidence for the Uí Chaím lordship within Fir Maige itself. Here, the tuath of Eóganacht Glennamnach and its immediate dependencies comprised in total nealy half of the eastern moiety of the tríucha céad of Fir Maige over which the Uí Chaím were immediate lords. At the same time the western moiety was held of the Uí Chaím by mesne-lords, the Uí Dubhagáin (the historical representative of Fir Maige Féne), thus placing the entire tríucha céad, an extensive area comprising the entire north-eastern portion of Co. Cork and the Anglesborough/Kilbehenny area of Co. Limerick, under the lordship of Uí Chaím.[35] Lack of evidence denies certain knowledge of the situation here before 1100, but, in light of the evidence adduced above for the continuing importance in Munster politics of Eóganacht Glennamnach in the tenth and eleventh centuries, the firm likelihood must be that the Eóganacht Glennamnach were in general overlords of the local kings of Fir Maige. It is interesting to note that, while the terms 'king of Fir Muighe' and 'king of Glennamnain' can be found side by side in the earlier annals, relating respectively to the ancestors of the Uí Dubhagáin and Uí Chaím, the Finguine Ua Caoimh who died in 1135 was the last of his dynasty to use the style, 'king of Glennamnain'. His son and successor, Aedh, and his descendants for nearly a century after, use the style 'king of Fir Muige'.[36]

This brings us to the question of the extent of Uí Chaím lordship beyond the boundaries of Fermoy. While there is no direct evidence to indicate the extent, if any, of this, I believe that the extent of the cult of St Colmán of Cloyne, indicated by the shape of the diocese of Cloyne, may well indicate the actual area of Eóganacht Glennamnach mesne-

---

35 Power 1932, 45–9. **36** *A Tig* 640; *CS* 641, 1012; *AFM* 640, 843, 1013, 1161; *FIA* 908 (p. 211); *ALC* 1014. In the earlier period it is clear the respective titles 'rí Fer Maige' and 'rí (Eóganacht) Glennamnach' were used in a dynastic rather than territorial sense. It was only in the twelfth century that Fir Maige won out as the territorial appelation for the tríucha céad.

lordship in Desmuma during periods of the tenth and eleventh centuries, especially bearing in mind the continuing strength of the dynasty in this period. Such a conclusion is primarily based on the long and symbiotic relationship between the Síl Cathail/Eóganacht Glennamnach lordship and the cult of St Colmán, both of which, it will be noted, experienced the same south-westward movement over several centuries and which, as we have seen, has its roots in the sixth century relationship between saint and royal patron.

CHAPTER SEVEN

Literary evidence of Colmán's cult

7.1 Colmán in the Martyrologies and Corpus Sanctorum

In the present chapter I propose to adduce and discuss all subsequent references to the cult of Colmán in chronological order. The next series of evidences to be considered in relation to this cult is that to be found in the Irish calendars or martyrologies. The earliest of these, the so-called *Felire of Óengus* and the Martyrology of Tallaght, are closely related and can both be dated to the first half of the ninth century.[1] The former, under 24 November, simply gives *mac Lenini*, to which the twelfth-century glossator has added *i. ó Chlúain húma in Huib Liathan hi Mumain Colmán nomen eius* 'of Cloyne in Uí Liatháin in Munster, Colmán was his name'. *Tallaght*, under 15 October, has *nativitas Colmain meic Lenín*, this entry referring to the saint's *nativitas* or birthday, unlike that of *Óengus*, which refers to the saints *natalis* or date of death. The much later Martyrology of Gorman, dating to around 1170, records *Colmán mac leir Lénéin* under 24 November, which the editor translates 'Colmán, Léinín's pious son', to which the glossator has added 'of Cluain Uamach in Uí Liatháin'.[2] Under 6 March both *Óengus* and *Tallaght* list *Inghena Lenini* 'the daughters of Léinín', to which a glossator to the former adds *ó Cell ingen leir Lenini in Huí Briuin Cualann*, (Killiney, Co. Dublin). Under the same date *Gorman* has *Nert inghen leir Lenin* which the editor translates 'the virtue of Léinín's active daughters'.

A source of perhaps similar date and which again refers to both Colmán and his sisters is the body of saintly genealogies or pedigrees often referred to as the *Corpus Genealogiarum Sanctorum*. There is disagreement among scholars as to the dating of this material, with Ó Riain,

---

1 Best and Lawlor; Stokes 1905; Ó Riain 1990, 26–35. 2 Stokes 1895.

who has edited the *Corpus*, suggesting an eleventh century date while Ó Corráin would attribute a ninth century date to the bulk of the material.[3] We have already noticed (3.1) a derivative relationship between the late pedigree of Mac Léinín as contained in the *Corpus* and that of Trinity MS 1298 which has been dated to before AD 700 and a similar relationship can be found in pedigree material relating to Finbarr of Cork.[4] Accordingly, I would tend to accept a ninth or tenth century dating for at least some of the pedigrees of the *Recensio Maior*, regardless of the certainly later date of the earliest surviving recension of the text.

Immediately following upon Colmán's pedigree in the *Corpus* occurs mention of his sisters.

> *Secht n-ingena Lénine: Aiglend, Machain* [or *Macha*], *Luiden, Druiden, Lucell, Rimthech, Briget. Et óga in sin uile cenmotha Aglend a hoenur.*[5]

The last sentence may be translated 'and all were virgins apart from Aglend'. This is to be understood in light of the references to her in a document titled 'On the Mothers of the Saints', which can hardly be much later in date of composition than the *Recensio Maior*. In this source Aglend is made the spouse of Eochaid, a dynast of the Southern Uí Néill segment, Cenél Láegaire, and mother of Colum or Colmán Midísil, Lugaid and Fintan. Of these three the first two were themselves saints, Colmán Midísil being associated with Ros Glandai *alias* Domnach Mór Maige Imchláir, the present Donoghmore, Co. Tyrone, and Lugaid with Tír Dá Chraebh or Teernacreeve, Co. Westmeath. Colmán's pedigree is recorded in the *Recensio Maior* while both saints are commemorated in the martyrologies.[6] While there is no way to test the historicity of these references is it a complete coincidence that Mac Léinín is credited with composition of a eulogy to Áed Sláne, a king of the same people? The sense in which 'virgin' is used above in reference to the remaining sisters is that of having

---

3 *CSH* xvii–xviii; Ó Riain 1983, 24; Ó Corráin 1981a, 330ff.   **4** Ó Corráin 1998, 197.   **5** *CSH* 215.2.   **6** Ibid., 160.1, 2, 349, 690.3, 722.31. Colmán Midísil is celebrated in the calendars on 6 September and Lugaid on 31 January.

taken a vow of celibacy and thus living a monastic life, presumably at Killiney, although more recent tradition, whatever its value, associates two of these, Briget and Machain, with church sites in Co. Cork (App. B).

7.2 Colmán interred at Cloyne

The next reference to our saint which can be securely dated occurs in the annals now known as the *Fragmentary Annals of Ireland*. These are of mid-eleventh-century provenance and appear to have been composed in Ossrige. The reference to Mac Léinín occurs in a long narrative section *sub anno* 908 concerning Cormac mac Cuillenáin, the famous king-bishop of Cashel and Munster. This tells how, after Cormac was fatally wounded at Belach Mugna, 'he ordered that his body be brought to Cluain Uama ... he was very desirous of being interred at Cluain Uama with MacLénín'.[7] This reference is of interest for a number of reasons. Though written nearly a century and a half after the events described, the Ossrige scribe may well have been drawing on a genuine tradition given that at the time the annal was composed Ossrige and Eóganacht Chaisil were close allies. While the theme of burial in a cemetery first occupied by a famous saint is a common one in Irish hagiography this reference is of greater interest in that it suggests that, even some half century after Síl Cathail had been marginalized by Eóganacht Chaisil, Colmán Mac Léinín remained – and would remain for some time to come – a powerful patron-saint of the latter polity. It may even be that Eóganacht Chaisil still retained hereditary burial rights in Cloyne dating from the earlier period of Síl Cathail dominance.

7.3 Colmán as Eóganacht patron: Dalcassian propaganda

Nearly all references to Mac Léinín subsequent to that in *FAI*, down to the time of the Anglo-Norman invasion and beyond, can be grouped

7 *FIA* p. 153.

under two main themes. Firstly, we have that of powerful totem or patron saint of the Eóganacht and, secondly, that relating to his poetry. To treat firstly of the former, all of these references occur in the context of propaganda which, in time-honoured Irish fashion, sought to legitimise the rule of the usurper dynasty of Dál Cais to the kingship of Munster in the face of the traditional Eóganacht claims. While these show the continued role of Mac Léinín as patron of the Eóganacht, more importantly, they provide powerful evidence for the continued potency of the cult of Mac Léinín – first demonstrated in the early eighth-century tract *Conall Corc* – in legitimizing the rule of the incumbent king of Munster, more, one suspects, in the quasi-druidical sense of the *magus* as representative of the pagan divine than as Christian saint as representative of the Christian God.

The first of these references which can be dated with some certainty occurs in the Dalcassian propaganda tract, *Cogadh Gaedhel re Gallaibh*, which has been dated to the period 1103 x 1113. The relevant passage – in translation – has Mac Léinín prophesying eternal rule in Munster for the descendants of Cormac Cas, the fictional eponym of Dál Cais, in the following terms:

> As was said by the religious, the prophet, the poet (*an credal ocus in fiadh ocus in file*), viz. Colmán Mac Léinín
>> The family of Cormac Cas, of many deeds,
>> To them shall belong the noble sovereignty
>> Except three, until Flann comes[8]

This theme is greatly expanded in a narrative which, although it only survives in a redaction of the early eighteenth century, is clearly based, in part at least, on a much earlier exemplar or exemplars, probably of twelfth-century date, and which, in spite of being largely unhistorical, has formed the basis for much of the little historiography written on the saint in modern times. This narrative, from the Book of Munster, cen-

---

8 Todd 1867, 73. For the dating of *Cogadh* see Ní Mhaonaigh.

tres around an incident set in Colmán's period involving a dispute between Aodh mac Conaill of the Dál Cais and Aodh mac Crimthainn of the Eóganacht for the kingship of Munster. It is worth giving a full translation of the relevant parts of this narrative.

> This Aodh mac Conaill mac Eochach Balldeirg was the first person of the Dál Cais to receive the kingdom of Munster after the [coming of] the faith, even though the Eóganacht historians do not list him; but the following account of what happened when Aodh mac Crimthainn i.e. the father of Finguine and Failbe Flann, made submission to Aodh mac Conaill at Carn in Rig in Mag Feimin, shows nevertheless that it was true. On that occasion Aodh mac Crimthainn arrived into the house of Aodh mac Conaill mac Eochadh Balldeirg and there and then Aodh mac Conaill was enkinged and he took the hostages of Munster. Both Brendan and Colmán mac Léinín the poet found themselves at this gathering and they became guarantors for Aodh mac Conaill …
>
> Then Brendan witnessed the service of angels over Lothra and told that to the king. And Brendan sent a disciple to find out what happened there and along with him Mac Léinín as a witness from the king. Indeed [some] people say that it was Cuimíne Fada whom Brendan sent there; I do not know if that is true, since Cuimíne was born twenty years after Brendan died, and Cuimíne had not fully ten years [of age] when Mac Léinín died. Moreover Mac Léinín had been thirty years a bishop when he died, and he had not [yet] changed from his lay life when that meeting took place.
>
> However, the disciples and Mac Léinín reached the loch, and they found the shrine of Ailbe there and Mac Léinín took it, and they saw the dead *giolla* in the loch, and they took the shrine in the form of a chest, since God had drowned them [the thieves] over it. After that the shrine went to Brendan and he recognized in the man of poetry that the favour of God was on him. And he said, moreover, that it was not proper that the hands that had held the holy relics should ever be polluted. Because of this Mac

Léinín offered himself to God and Brendan, and Brendan blessed him, and his name was changed to Colmán mac Léinín. As Brendan said:

> Colmán of Cluain Uamha
> A feather of gold
> A powerful victory's boast
> A part of the King of pure heaven's sun
> A distinguished noble
> Royal quatrained

Then Mac Léinín said to Aodh mac Conaill the king: 'Not less do we need to receive reward, because we have given up the art through which we could have received reward'. The king said: 'That which I would give you for your poetry is what you will later receive for the sake of God.'

It was then that the king released him from taxes from himself and from every king who should take Cashel for ever. And the same to Brendan. And Mac Léinín and Brendan are guarantors that this account is true, and it would be called a possession (*comarbus*) from him, and the high-king of Cashel at this happening was Aodh mac Conaill, etc., and Aodh mac Conaill took Brendan with him to his house in hope of receiving his blessings there. So that it was then that Brendan made this blessing in gratitude, etc.[9]

The reference to a meeting in the second paragraph of this account between Brendan and Mac Léinín is to be understood as a reference to a meeting between these two as narrated in one of Brendan's Lives, which can be translated as follows.

> When he [Brendan] went to consult his foster-mother, Ita, she said … that he should learn the rules of the saints of Ireland. 'Do not,' she said, 'learn of women or virgins lest they be reproached

9 Ó Donnchadha, 88–91.

regarding it. Go, and there shall meet thee on the road a well-known well-born *laech*.' And it happened that this *laech* was Mac Léinín. So when Brendan set out Mac Léinín met him. 'Repent' said Brendan to him, 'for God is calling thee, and thou shalt be his own son from henceforth.' Colmán mac Léinín then turned to the Lord, and a church was built by him forthwith.[10]

In this excerpt from a late (thirteenth-century) source *laech* can be understood as warrior, a misreading which, no doubt, gave rise to the reference to Colmán in a fourteenth-century poem of Thomond provenance, when, as *Mac Leinin an gai géir gloin* 'Mac Léinín of the keen bright spear' he is listed among the saints who will come to Senán's aid.[11] While these accounts are of little value for our saint's life they contain valuable material relating to his cult in the period around the twelfth century. While it would be desirable to have to hand the earlier account or accounts on which the *Book of Munster* narrative is based, these do not seem to have survived. It would appear that the later scribe has faithfully reproduced the thrust of the polemic or propaganda underlying these sources, which allow us to firmly locate these in an early twelfth-century milieu. Politics in Munster in this period was dominated by the division of the province between the Uí Briain and Meic Carthaig and our exemplar(s) belong to the propaganda war which waged alongside the martial war between these two powerful regnal families. The central thrust of this propaganda was aimed at justifying the claims of the Uí Briain to the kingship of Munster in the face of counter-propaganda by the Meic Carthaig in justification of their historically more valid claims. In a society in which the right to rule – in theory at least – was allowed solely in a context of descent from a legitimate royal caste of long standing the Uí Briain, in truth, mere usurpers of inferior descent, were forced to compose a fictional descent making them an early offshoot of the Eóganacht and thus as entitled to royal rule as their Meic Carthaig rivals. A key element in this fictional descent was the person of Aodh mac Conaill, who

10 Plummer 1922, 47.   11 Sharpe 1991, 24–5; Plummer 1915, 28–9.

was claimed to have once held the kingship of Munster and thus to legitimize the right of his Uí Briain descendants to such rule.[12] The historically literate scribes tasked with this function cleverly intervove historical figures into their composition in order to lend weight to the fiction
that Aodh mac Conaill was an historical personage. Moreover, they delib-
erately chose saints, especially Mac Léinín, with long standing Eóganacht
connexions, thus cleverly reversing the actual position and, in the tradition of all good propaganda, turning truth into falsehood.

The core of the picture of Mac Léinín as given in both accounts
above is historically accurate: a poet with a connexion with royal Cashel
who converted to a life of religion. The likely truth of this connexion is
reversed, making Mac Léinín's original royal benefactor a Dalcassian
rather than Eóganacht ancestor, showing that the author must have
known the substance of the account of the true connexion as given in
Conall Corc. Again, the chronology is right as Aod mac Crimthainn was
a contempory of Mac Léinín. Of the saints introduced into the account
two, in addition to Mac Léinín, have Eóganacht connexions. Ailbe
founded the monastery of Emly, certainly the most important monastery
in Eóganacht dominated Munster, while Ruadán of Lorrha, made to
feature in that section of the narrative immediately preceding that quoted
above, was a saint of some importance to the Meic Carthaig in the
twelfth century.[13] Thus the propagandist seeks to legitimize anti-
Eóganacht claims by using three saints with powerful Eóganacht connexions and symbolism. The relationship between Mac Léinín and St
Brendan as portrayed in both the *Book of Munster* account and in the
contemporary Life should also be viewed as part of the propagandist's
agenda. Brendan was patron of both Ardfert and Clonfert, both dioceses partly within or on the borders of the Uí Briain kingdom of
Thomond, and thus may be seen, at least in a twelfth-century context,
as a Dalcassian saint. Here the author would seem to be providing a
hagiographical parallel to that of the secular polity in which the Uí Briain
are seen as dominant over the Meic Carthaig, by making Mac Léinín

12 Ó Donnchadha, 86, 88–9, 91, 296–7. **13** Ó Riain 1985, 8.

subservient in calling to Brendan, and thus his spiritual son. This association between our subject and St Brendan is most unlikely to have any
historical merit whatsoever. The latter has a long association with polities inimical to those associated with Mac Léinín: firstly the kingdom
of Ciarraige Luachra in Iarmuma and later the Uí Briain. I might conclude this section with the observation that the use made of Mac Léinín
in twelfth-century Dalcassian propaganda must reflect, in addition to
his historical value as an Eóganacht totem, the contemporary power of
his cult in part of the rival twelfth-century kingdom of Desmuma.

7.4 Colmán as poet in historical memory

To turn to those references within the theme of poetry, these illustrate
the longevity of the powerful image of Colmán Mac Léinín as virtually
first among Ireland's poets and provide an interesting aside to the purely
cultic details of his sainthood. The tenth-century *Cormac's Glossary* contains a number of references to words used in some of the poems attributed to Mac Léinín, thus giving quite early evidence connecting this
poetry to the saint.[14] From the eleventh or twelfth century comes a poem
on the Saints of Ireland, attributed to Cuimín, which says about Colmán

> *Carais Colmán caomh Cluana*
> *filidheacht tre chóir séisi*
> *gach áon do mholadh gan locht*
> *ni thiged olc da éisi*[15]

> 'Dear Colmán of Cloyne
> loved poetry through skilful arrangement
> Whoever was praised without fault [by Colmán]
> evil would not come after him'

Once again we have the recurrent theme of the power of bardic rather
than saintly benediction. Finally, we might note the praise poem to

14 Stokes 1868, 10, 42. **15** Stokes 1897, 64.

Colmán written by Gofraidh Fionn Ó Dálaigh (*obit* 1387), probably a native of Desmuma.[16] This composition begins

A Cholmáin mhóir mheic Léinín	'Great Colmán, son of Léinín,
A bhinnegnaidh bhaisghléimhín	melodius sage of smooth bright hand
Grádh dhuid as dú d'Ibh Dálaigh	the O Dalys are bound to love thee
Tú ar gcuid dona Colmánaibh	thou are our share of the Colmáns'

In this poem Ó Dálaigh makes Colmán the fosterer and teaching master of Dálach, eponymous ancestor of the Uí Dhálaigh, thus claiming at one stroke the mantle of ancient saint and *fili* with the corresponding blessings of both vocations. Uí Dhálaigh, certainly the single greatest bardic sept of Gaelic Ireland, appear to descend from the Corcu Ádaim of Meath, a descent perhaps unknown to Gofraidh, and it is probable that this association between this famous *ollamhan* sept and one of the 'fathers of Irish literature' as outlined in the poem is merely clever poetic artifice rather than genuine tradition, in spite of the associations adduced above between Colmán and Meath (5.2). What is clear from this poem is the continued reverence paid to Colmán by the bardic schools nearly eight centuries after he had lived and probably composed.

7.5 *Colmán in* Beatha Molaca

One final probable reference to our subject is noteworthy. In a late *betha* of St Molaca of Templemolaga and Aghacross, composed in the twelfth or thirteenth century, one Saint Mo Cholmóg makes a cameo appearance.[17] Mo Cholmóg is, of course, a hypocoristic form of Colmán. In this narrative Molaca and Mo Cholmóg arrive in the house of Cathail mac Aedha, king of Munster, just as his wife has died in giving birth to a son. Hearing the keening of the household upon the death, the clerics also hear the piercing cries of the newborn infant, crying 'like a pup

---

16 Bergin 1918.   **17** O'Keeffe, 16–17; Ó Riain 1997a, 33.

without its mother', as Mo Cholmóg says, to which Molaca replies, 'that will be his name'. Hence the infant is named Cú cen Mathair, and goes on to become king of Munster in his own right. The subject matter and chronology of this narrative suggests that this Mo Cholmóg represents Colmán Mac Léinín. The royal line in question are the Síl Cathail, whose association with Mac Léinín must have been known to the scribe, who must also have been aware of the annals which record the birth of Cú cen Mathair in 603/4, within the computed lifespan of Mac Léinín.[18] This cameo appearance probably owes more to the ecclesiastical politics of the period when the *betha* was composed – a theme which will be explored below – than to any genuine tradition linking the birth of the king with our saint, although of course we cannot be sure of this in light of the well documented linkages adduced above.

One further connexion is to be found in the life of Findchú of Brí Gobann, dated to the same period. While this makes no overt reference to our subject the author of this *betha* was certainly aware of the ancient connexions between Mac Léinín and Síl Cathail as he uses these as a model for a fictional account of Findchú's early life. In this the saint meets with and allies himself with Coirpre Crom in exactly the same way that MacLéinín is portrayed as doing in the sources, even down to sharing martial exploits with the king and a royal donation of Brí Gobann to the saint. Of course Brí Gobann was both in the diocese of Cloyne and the territory of Fir Maige and so the author of the *betha* had every incentive for stealing MacLéinín's story.[19]

18 *A Tig* 603/4; *CS, AU* 604. **19** Stokes 1890, 97.

CHAPTER EIGHT

The church of *Cluain Uama*

8.1 The ecclesiastical town of Cluain Uama: *foundation and early development*

Before treating of the history of the cult of Mac Léinín it is first necessary to outline that of his chief foundation at Cloyne. Swan sees no reason not to 'accept the general accuracy of dating attribution for monastic foundation'[1] and, as we have seen above, by at least the early eighth century Colmán Mac Léinín was considered to have been the founder of a church at Cloyne or Cluain Uama, an event which can be dated by an agreement of the evidence to the third quarter of the sixth century. It has been noticed that most important church centres were founded either on the site of a pre-existing pagan centre of worship, such as Kildare and Armagh, or as cenobitic foundations on waste or uninhabited land, the latter category usually bearing the toponym *cluain*, 'raised meadow surrounded by bog'.[2] This is a perfect description of the location of Cluain Uama, where a low-lying (and cave riddled) limestone plateau in a shallow synclinal valley was once surrounded on three sides by marshland. From this it would appear that Mac Léinín founded a monastic settlement on virgin soil at Cloyne. We cannot be sure that this was his chief foundation but, as we have seen above (7.2), in the eleventh-century Cloyne was believed to have been his burial place and it seems probable that Cloyne was the principal residence of Mac Léinín. All tradition agrees that Mac Léinín was a monk and it would seem that he founded a cenobitic monastery here that may, as we have already speculated, have maintained a school of *filidecht* and jurisprudence from its foundation onwards.

1 Swan, 100. 2 Hughes 1972, 74–5; Doherty 1985, 52.

The surviving annals are especially poor in south Munster history and Cloyne fares even worst than the other foundations in the area. We have a good list of annals relating to Cloyne from the ninth century and then a near two-century gap until the 1060s, after which annals once again survive for Cloyne. We are fortunate in having one earlier source, the guarantor list for the proclamation of *Cáin Adomnáin*, generally accepted as authentic and datable to 697 although preserved in a later recension. This document twice mentions Eochaid, abbot of *Clúan Húama*, once in the guarantor list and once in a much more select list of those giving security for the law's decree on the emancipation of women. While the identification, appended to the list, of the guarantors has been shown to be datable to a period perhaps one or two generations after the actual promulgation in 697 and on occasion to be incorrect,[3] the prominence of Eochaid in the document suggests that his given title is correct and, at the very least, gives a firm indication of the importance of the church of Cloyne in the early eighth century as only one other church from southern Munster can be shown with certainty to have featured in the list (Cork).

These references from the late seventh-century suggest that Cloyne was then an important monastery and ecclesiastical centre if we are to judge by the prominence of its abbot. Shortly after the beginning of annals for Cloyne, in 821, we find an annal *sub anno* 885 which records the slaying of both its abbot and prior by the Norsemen. This is the first of several annals recording raids or damage to Cloyne, while there is also evidence for an earlier Norse raid of *c.*824. In 978 Cloyne was ravaged by the Ossrige, in 1088 plundered by Diarmait Ua Briain and in 1137 'its houses and churches' were burned.[4] These entries must be understood in light of the multidimensional roles of the large ecclesiastical centre, which, in addition to its pastoral functions, had also become secular town and commercial hub for its hinterland. It would seem from the annal of 885 that the monastery of Cloyne must have acquired the accre-

3 Meyer 1905, 13, 17; Note no. 13, Chapter 6.   4 *AFM* 885, 1137; *A Tig* 977 (=978); *AI* 1088.2; Todd 1867, 29.

tion of an urban settlement by that date, for the Norsemen were principally driven by the acquisition of material wealth and slaves.

8.2 Cluain Uama: *topography*

Doherty considers that the urban development of what had been originally isolated cenobitic foundations was due to the advanced technological agricultural methods of the monks, especially by the use of the horizontal water-mill and the heavy plough. Such methods resulted in a grain surplus which in turn attracted a large population over time, as also did the gravitational pull of an established centre in contrast to the peripatetic nature of the institution of kingship. Over time the core ecclesiastical ceremonial complex became surrounded by public buildings and open spaces, secular residential areas and a dedicated market site. Doherty suggests a chronology for this process which sees the monasteries already acting as commercial redistributive centres – and presumably with secular urban settlement – by no later than the early 800s, and culminating in the picture of the fully developed monastic town as given below by the early to mid-tenth century.[5] His description of such towns is worth quoting as what we might envisage as once having existed at Cloyne:

> (Irish monastic towns) clearly had large populations, are divided into districts, have a literate elite, some of whom are administrators, are at the centre of large estates, and have properties in other parts of the country; they have large public buildings and monuments, public open spaces, streets, some of which are paved and on the outskirts they have a market place.[6]

The annal of 885 suggests that Cloyne was well on the way to such a state of development in that year, while that of 1137, with its reference to the

5 Doherty 1980, 81–2; 1985, 55–67. **6** 68.

common medieval phenomenon of catastrophic urban fire destruction, confirms such a development.

In an important study Swan has shown that Irish monastic or ecclesiastical towns had a common 'consistent and orderly pattern' of development, some of which can be seen at Cloyne. In general the early Irish ecclesiastical town featured a double circular enclosure pattern, with an outer enclosure of average diameter of *c.*400 meters surrounding an inner enclosure of average diameter of *c.*150 meters, in which the sacred ecclesiastical complex of churches and cemeteries was located. In general the round tower was located on or near the boundary of the inner enclosure at the western end of the ecclesiastical complex while the market place was usually located within or just outside the outer enclosure near the main entrance or gate to the entire town, usually located east of the sacred complex. Key access points in the complex were usually decorated with carved stone crosses, one of the most prominent of which would be located at the market place.[7]

Several of these features may be discerned at Cloyne, where the settlement occupied the western end of a low and narrow limestone ridge or plateau some miles in length rising from marshy ground (see Map 1). Unfortunately this important and ancient settlement has been mostly neglected to-date by the science of archaeology and one eagerly awaits redress. In the absence of such investigation one must rely, when engaged on the task of reconstructing something of the extent of the ancient ecclesiastical town, on the few surviving surface features. In the case of Cloyne the general east-west axis of such towns as noted by Swan appears to have been replaced by a north-south one, due no doubt both to the terrain in question and the departure of the major road linking Cloyne to the outside world in a northerly direction from the northern edge of the ridge. It seems likely that the outer enclosure here was set on the edge of the limestone plateau to north, west and south. The major north-south axis of the settlement can probably be measured by the width of the ridge here along the same axis, approximately 400 metres. At least

7 Swan, 98–100.

part of the line of the original inner enclosure may be discerned by the quadrant line of the ancient lane that borders the cathedral and grave yard to east and south. If the location of the Round Tower at Cloyne – at the western end of the inner enclosure – follows the general pattern in such matters this would give a west-east diameter of 150 metres for the inner enclosure. Both figures agree well with the average sizes of such enclosures as noted by Swan. Finally we should note the possible identification of an erstwhile Celtic or Anglo-Norman market cross near the Litton Fountain in Rock Street, 180 metres north of the cathedral. A location north rather than east of the inner enclosure for the market place would fit well with the topography of Cloyne.[8]

8.3 The cult of Mac Léinín and the paruchia of Cloyne

In almost all cases important ecclesiastical towns had at core a church complex under the patronage of an important saint whose cult was closely associated with and promoted by the church in question. In the case of Cloyne this saint of course was Colmán Mac Léinín, and we must now turn to the question of the territorial extent of his cult and of the *paruchia* of his church of Cloyne, and the history of both over the entire period of the Early Irish Church. Our task here is made particularly difficult by the dearth of annalistic and other evidence for the period of the Early Irish Church from South Munster.

The earliest annal concerning Cloyne is that recording the death of its abbot, Cu Caéch, in 821. This is followed by the obit of abbot Mael Cobha Ua Faeláin in 859, abbot Niall mac Donngaile in 871 and abbot Fergal mac Fínnechta and prior Uamanán mac Cérén in 885.[9] After this there is a near two-century silence concerning Cloyne in the annals. The 871 annal also describes Niall mac Donngaile as abbot of Cúil Collainge, now Coole near Castlelyons. This church appears to have been founded late in the eighth century[10] and lay about 18 miles north of Cloyne,

---

8 Ibid., 99–100; Zajac et al., 32–4. 9 *AFM* 821 857, 885; *AU* 858 (= 859); *AI* 871. 10 *AI* 800.

although in the same kingdom or polity, Uí Liatháin (at least in 871). This entry suggests that Cloyne had already come to dominate this lesser church, from which we may draw the implication that Cloyne already possessed a *paruchia* that, at the very least, consisted of much of the territory of Uí Liatháin. From this early reference to Cloyne's overlordship to the picture presented in the early years of the Anglo-Norman period, when the diocese of Cloyne is found in possession of many thousands of acres throughout its large diocese, little detailed evidence survives. Fortunately the pattern of distribution of the cult of St Colmán and associated cults within Co. Cork helps us to push back the picture significantly earlier, for it must be a given that these cults had developed to their fullest extent before the carve up of the *paruchia* of Cloyne at the synod of Ráith Breasail in 1111 – such an extensive cult infiltration can hardly have blossomed in the short period between the birth of the 'reformed' diocese of Cloyne and the Anglo-Norman invasion which brought its own cults with it – and therefore the distribution of these cults, at the very least, must represent a picture of the extent of the *paruchia* of Cloyne datable to the late eleventh century (see Map 2). As can be seen from this map, dedications to Colmán and his family occur throughout the area of the diocese of Cloyne, suggesting that by the late eleventh century the *paruchia* of Cloyne equalled, more or less, the area of the diocese as revealed in early thirteenth-century records. A further source of value for the extent of the early *paruchia* of Cloyne is the pattern of surname distribution among the betagh or unfree population of the cross-lands of the diocese as revealed in thirteenth- and fourteenth-century records (8.4 below). This pattern mirrors closely the geographical extent of cult dedication to the saint and his family, further reinforcing my point above identifying the area of the eleventh-century *paruchia* with that of the later diocese. Incidentally, a similar pattern of agreement can be found operating in relation to the cult distribution of St Finbarr and the extent of the diocese of Cork. (Appendix B). This is not to claim that the entire body of the cross-lands of Anglo-Norman Cloyne had belonged to the pre-invasion church and its *paruchia*. The process by which the *termonn* lands of the Irish Church passed into the

hands of the bishoprics of the Anglo-Norman period is not fully understood. What seems clear is that, given the evidence for the distribution
of the cult of Colmán and associates and that of surname distribution
of the *manaig* population, the pre-Norman church of Cloyne certainly
owned a significant portion of what later became the cross-lands of its
Anglo-Norman successor.

Within Cloyne diocese there had existed a number of lesser but still
significant churches, infrequently mentioned in the annals. Tullylease
and Coole do find some mention while the significance of Brigown is
attested by reference to its large *termonn* in the topographical tract,
Crichad an Chaoilli, its erstwhile round tower, and a ninth-century
Viking raid. Donoughmore must also have been a major church. Its onomastic character (*Domnach Mór Mitíne*) suggests it to have been a very
early 'free-church' and mother-church of its territory, an ecclesiastical
foundation without any monastic associations.[11] Whenever it came under
the sway of Cloyne it may have brought with it substantial scattered possessions in its eponymous territory of Múscraige Mitíne. When and how
Cloyne extended its ecclesiastical lordship over these churches and their
territories does not appear, apart from that of Coole. It is likely that the
growth of Cloyne's power was facilitated and supported by its principal
lay-patrons, Síl Cathail/Eóganacht Glennamnach, and in the vagaries
of the power of the latter we may see some reflections of that of Cloyne.
The tuath of Eóganacht Glennamnach, which, as we have seen above,
was the principal royal demesne of the lineage since at least the early
eighth century had, as its chief church, that of *Ceall Aenamhna*
(Killeenemer).[12] This church, along with its surrounding lands, is, not
surprisingly, later found in possession of the see of Cloyne and it seems
likely that this came about by a donation from its Eóganacht kings to
the church of Cloyne in the same way that we know, for instance, that
such similar donations were made to the church of Kells (Ceannanus
Mór).[13] Furthermore, the absence of reference in *Crichad an Chaoilli* to

---

11 *AI* 800, 871, 1059.6; *AFM* 839; *MIA* 1152.4; Power 1932, 46–7; Flanagan, 25–31; Sharpe 1992,
94–5; Todd 1867, 15. 12 Power 1932, 46; *PRC* 182 (n. 106). 13 Mac Niocaill, 104.

any hereditary clergy in this church suggests that it may have been served by chaplains from Cloyne. The pre-Norman association between Cloyne and Killeenemer is further supported by the results of my survey of the betagh population of Cloyne (8.4).

Something of further relevance here may be found in the subsequent pattern of landholding in the Anglo-Norman diocese of Cloyne. The temporalities of the see were organized into five separate manors: Cloyne, Coole, Killeenemer, Kilmaclenine and Donoughmore (Map 4). In each case the lands comprised in these manors lay within a single cantred, all five cantreds together comprising the entire area of the diocese.[14] There is clear evidence that these cantreds in turn were descended from the pre-Norman native administrative division, the *tricha cet*.[15] Is the continuum in administrative divisions paralleled in the case of the church lands? Cloyne, Coole and Donoughmore were certainly the principal churches in their respective *tríucha* while, as the chief church of the principal *tuath* of Fir Maige, the same can be said of Killeenemer. While the pre-Norman sources are silent concerning Kilmaclenine, its very derivation, from *Ceall Mhic Léinín*, indicates it to have been an important local centre of the patronal cult, a position it may have held for some centuries prior to the invasion. Further confirmation of this may be found in evidence which suggests that Kilmaclenine and Cloyne shared some of the same hereditary *manaig* families (8.4). In addition it will be noted that, in general, the area of the five cantreds of the diocese was paralleled ecclesiastically by corresponding rural deaneries. If this ruri-decanal structure is of similar origin to that of the diocese of Meath then these deaneries must have been based on earlier local or subservient bish-oprics, as discussed more fully below in section 9.4.

I have already illustrated the twelfth-century power of the Uí Chaím in a local context (6.3). While the dearth of evidence precludes certainty as to the actual extent of this area of what might be termed mesne-lord-ship, it is not an unreasonable speculation to suggest that this might have comprised, in addition to their native *tricha cet* of Fir Maige, the adja-

---

14 *PRC* 2–80. **15** See my 'Cantred and Tríucha Céad', forthcoming.

cent territories of Uí Liatháin and Uí Meic Caille – the latter included Cloyne – to the south, where, as has been shown already (6.1), the Síl Cathail ancestors of the Uí Chaím certainly exercised a significant over-lordship in earlier centuries. While the presence of these three *tríucha* in the *paruchia* of Cloyne is hardly surprising, given their long association with Síl Cathail and their patron, Colmán, that of the western *tríucha* of Múscraige Mitíne and Múscraige Ua nDonnagáin is certainly so. I would suggest that this inclusion is also the result of these territories being part of the mesne-lordship of Uí Chaím, which would in turn have sponsored Colmán's cult here. If this was indeed the case it provides a *terminus a quo* for the expansion of the cult and *paruchia* of Colmán here for, as long as the east/west division of Munster continued, one can hardly imagine a cult associated with the leading kings of Aurmuma being welcomed across the border in Iarmuma. I suspect that the dual occurrences of the collapse of this east/west divide after AD 800 and the relegation to local from provincial kingship of Síl Cathail/Eóganacht Glennamnach resulted in a westwards expansion of power by this dynasty just as it began to be pushed southwards from the northern limits of its area of lordship around Emly. The annalistic reference of 828 to the *muinter* of Cork and their Uí Echach allies suffering what appears to have been a defeat at the hands of the Múscraige Mitíne may reflect this change of overlordship here, and in turn reflect advances by Eóganacht Glennamnach against the hitherto locally dominant Uí Echach in a dual lay/ecclesiastical shift in lordship.[16] The south-westwards movement experienced by the polity of Síl Cathail appears to be matched by that of Colmán's cult. As demonstrated in the *Conall Corc* tale, the churches of Erry and Killenaule, both lying east of Cashel, bore dedications to Colmán in the early eighth century. There is no later history of such a dedication associated with either church, or with any other church in Tipperary, and it would seem that as the power of Síl Cathail waned in this area so too did the cult of Colmán mac Léinín.[17]

---

16 *AI* 828. **17** The parish of Colman in Middlethird barony appears to derive from a dedication to Colomba (Sweetman, p. 281). It is possible, however, that holy wells dedicated both

Some further indications of relevance to the growth of the *paruchia* of Cloyne may be discerned in the pattern of church dedication in Cork. While such dedications cannot be dated it seems clear that they must pre-date the Anglo-Norman invasion and, in some cases at least, can be shown to be several centuries older. Dedications to local saints aside, it is those of non-local saints which suggest an interesting pattern. The pattern of dedications to the patronal saints, Finbarr and Colmán, strictly adheres to the later diocesan boundaries with no crossing over (Appendix B). In Cork dedications to Brendan, Carthach of Lismore and Gobbán, all saints with west Munster associations, occur, while in Cloyne, where most of the saints are homegrown or with local ethnic associations, Ruadán of Lorrha, a saint with both strong Eóganacht as well as Múscraige connexions, can be found in Fir Maige and Múscraige Mitíne.[18] Of particular interest is the dedication of Iniscarra Parish, which lies in Cloyne diocese and in the ancient territory of Múscraige Mitíne, to Senán of Inis Chathaig (Scattery), another west Munster saint. In a life of Senán Iniscarra is said to lie in the territory of Uí Echach, which may perhaps preserve a memory of the Uí Echach dominance of Múscraige Mitíne as referred to above.[19] While there are some further exceptions to this dedicatory pattern its general thrust may perhaps reflect some memory of the ancient ecclesiastical history of the area and the struggles between the *paruchiae* of Cork and Cloyne.

Thus the picture that emerges is one of an almost organic growth of the *paruchia* of Cloyne over several centuries, closely matching, in part, that of the area of political lordship of Síl Cathail/Eóganacht Glennamnach. Given the poor state of the sources for this area and period much about this growth must remain speculative. An early life of Carthach of Lismore, a date for which as early as the eighth century has been proposed by Sharpe, suggests that the church of Clondullane in the later diocese of Cloyne then lay in the *paruchia* of Lismore while mention in the same life of Rostellan, just west of Cloyne, also associ-

to Colmán and Brigit near Emly preserve memories of Mac Léinín's cult here (see Appendix B). **18** Brendan at Cannaway/Canovee, Carthach at Kilmoe, Gobbán at Kilgobban, and Ruadán at Aghinagh and Templerowan. **19** O'Hanlon, 227–9.

ates it with Carthach and thus Lismore. That such was indeed the case is suggested by the possession by Lismore of the parish of Kilworth, just north of Clondullane, as a detached portion surrounded wholly by the diocese of Cloyne until at least the fourteenth century.[20] It is likely that such references can be understood in light of the gradual growth of *paruchiae* over several centuries, resulting from the same centrifugal forces then evident in political life in Ireland. While over time more and more of the area represented by the later diocese of Cloyne would seem to have come under the lordship of that church the process must have been gradual and individual churches within the area of the later diocese must have, (like Kilworth), continued to represent detached portions of other *paruchiae*, just as we know to have been the case with those detached parts of the *paruchia* of Armagh, to give the most salient example of this phenomenon which can be found in several dioceses.[21] Indeed it is probable that the list of churches in Cloyne claimed by Cork in the late twelfth century, rather than representing a claim over the entire diocese of Cloyne by Cork as has been suggested, in fact represents just such a fragmentary extension of Cork's *paruchia* within Cloyne. It is noticeable that few of these claimed churches have any especial association with Cloyne while in one case, that of Killeagh and its patron, Ia, there is an actual hagiographical link with Finbarr.[22]

Another element in the growth of a *paruchia* around Cloyne must have been the size and wealth of the church itself. As the church (and town) of Cloyne grew in wealth and population it must have come to exercise an increasingly powerful sway in local politics. Cloyne was certainly to be numbered among those important church centres which could and often did field an army drawn from its *muinter* to settle affairs

---

20 Power 1914, 87, 110; Sharpe 1991, 385; Sweetman, 306. Per contra, Prof. Ó Riain (pers. comm.) would date this life to the early thirteenth century. 21 In 1216 the papacy issued a bull denying the archbishop of Armagh episcopal rights in parts of the diocese of Tuam, while a settlement of Armagh's claims to lands in various Connacht dioceses was agreed with the bishops of that province, in 1241. As late as 1351 the archdiocese of Armagh retained lands in the dioceses of Meath, Clogher, Elphin, Tuam, Annaghdown and Clonfert (Theiner, 295; *Ann. Conn.*, 1241.12; Sheehy, 185. I am indebted to Mr Kenneth Nicholls for assistance on this point). 22 Doble, 90; Thurston and Attwater, 34.

with neighbouring churches or polities, and some, at least, of the dynamic of *paruchia*-construction in the case of Cloyne may have involved simple conquest. It is hardly a coincidence that the entire cantred of McKille (Imokilly) and most of that of neighbouring Oglassyn, both of which together constituted the area of the pre-invasion polity of Uí Meic Caille, with an acreage of perhaps 100,000 acres, were numbered among the temporalities of the Anglo-Norman diocese.[23] From this it would seem that, in addition to an extended ecclesiastical *paruchia*, Cloyne ruled its immediate hinterland as a temporal petty-kingdom. (The reverse side of this coin was, of course, that leaders of the church of Cloyne were sometimes drawn from among the regnal families of Uí Meic Caille.) It may be noticed that, at the very least, this area equalled in size the similar area surrounding the church of Cork which we may safely surmise to have been part of its petty-kingdom in pre-invasion times.

8.4 *The* Manaig *families of Cloyne and its* paruchia

While no contemporary records of the *manaig* families of the *paruchia* of Cloyne survive we do have extensive evidence for those families holding in betaghry and gavillery on the cross-lands of the diocese during the thirteenth and fourteenth centuries. The terms *manaig* and *biataig* can refer to the same phenomenon but in distinct periods, that of the unfree or tied agricultural population associated with particular church lands. These were not necessarily 'serfs' as understood by the use of that term in the non-Irish feudal manorial context and would seem to have been agricultural workers and farmers of diverse social strata, all of whom were legally attached to a particular holding on an hereditary basis. There is abundant evidence that such tied populations were initially undisturbed by the arrival of the Anglo-Normans and continued to fulfill their social role for some generations after, and this is particularly true of such

---

23 *PRC* 2–20.

tenants on ecclesiastical lands. In the case of Cloyne we are fortunate in having substantial records relating to this class resident on the diocesan lands which therefore, I would suggest, offers some basis for assessing the pre-Norman *manaig* population of Cloyne.[24]

The social range occupied by such families is best illustrated in the case of the Uí Longáin. This sept are named among the 13 septs of *puri homines Sancti Colmani*, who 'belong to the church' (of Cloyne) in 1364. In 1198 'Ua Longáin of Uí Meic Caille' was slain at the instigation of one of the new Norman lords of McKille, yet the senior line of the sept continued to hold extensive lands just east of Cloyne, around Bohillane and Shanagarry, until becoming extinct in the male line around 1260. A portion of this estate was cross-land, and other members of the sept continued to occupy other cross-lands around Cloyne as betaghs or gavillers as recorded in 1364. Between 1275 and 1284 Alan Ua Longáin was bishop of Cloyne while another local member of the sept was a cattle-thief, as recorded in 1308.[25] The *termonn* of Cloyne, of course, had the largest *manaig*/betagh population in the ecclesiastical overlordship, and, if we are to judge by the extent of the colonial manor of Cloyne, the earlier *termonn* consisted of at least 10,000 acres. The evidence suggests, however, that some of these Cloyne *manaig* had settlements on other church estates within the *paruchia*.

Probably the most dramatic evidence concerns the O Molykannysh/ Molginnes sept, found in the thirteenth and fourteenth centuries on cross-lands at Lackeen near Kilmaclenine and in the latter century as *puri homines* at Cloyne and also at Coole. Another triple connexion involves the O Honyn/Hannon sept, who occur in Cloyne, Coole and Clenor in Western Fermoy, all in the fourteenth century. Staying with Fermoy, one O Leynan occurs in connexion with Killeenemer in the latter century. This appears to be the earlier Uí Laígenáin sept, an important ecclesiastical lineage, associated, as we shall see below, with the government of both Cloyne and Emly, where the sept originated. This ref-

---

24 This class are commemorated in Cloyne parish today in the townland of Farranamanagh, which remained in church possession into the nineteenth century. **25** *PRC* 18, 178 note 78.

erence is particularly interesting in view of the linkages discussed elsewhere in this study (6.1, 8.5) between Cloyne, Emly, and the Uí Chaím, lords of Killeenemer. Further evidence of Fermoy inclusion in the nexus of Colmán's cult is suggested by the presence as tenants on cross-land at Aghacross of the sept Uí Gilla Cholmáin during the thirteenth century. The name of this sept suggests an ancestor devoted to the veneration of the saint. Furthermore, it may not be a coincidence that the O Geveny surname occurs both among betaghs at Cloyne and at Aghacross. Similarly, O Dwyer occurs both at Cloyne and at Clenor. Finally, notice should be paid to the Uí Fhinn sept, who occur as betaghs around Cloyne and on cross-lands at Iniscarra in Muskerrymittine (to give the colonial version of the territorial designation). One of this sept was bishop of Cloyne 1247-64 and the surname is onomastically well attested around Cloyne itself.[26] These examples should be sufficient to indicate the probability of a strong pattern of linkage among the *manaig* population of these church estates in the pre-Norman period. The hub of these connexions, as one would expect, was Cloyne itself and this pattern suggests that most, if not all of the estates mentioned in this survey belonged to the diocese of Cloyne, at least in the immediate pre-invasion period. Indeed some of the sept associations occurring here, such as those at Aghacross, Killeenemer and Clenor, with their Eóganacht Áine (= Emly) and Dál Cais backgrounds, are suggestive of origins significantly earlier, perhaps from the paruchial period. (The results of this survey are illustrated in Map 3.)

8.5 Cloyne and Emly

So much for the *paruchia* of Cloyne. What of its relations with other churches? At the very least the term *paruchia* can safely be taken to denote the area of territorial dominance or lordship pertaining to a particular church. This late-latin word originally signified any area of ecclesiastical

---

26 Ibid., 14–18, 22–4, 32, 40, 50, 66–8, 72–4, 86–8, 108, 179 note 80, 186 note 123, 209 note 162.

jurisdiction, usually episcopal but later parochial.[27] In his study of this division in Munster Etchingham found evidence from the period before AD 1000 of the existence of particular *paruchiae*. The territory of Ciarraige was one such and appears to have been subject to the metropolitan over-lordship of the *paruchia* of Lismore, leading to the conclusion that, at least in the case of Lismore, a metropolitan authority was claimed 'over an aggregate of territorial jurisdictions, some contigious and some not'.[28] Something similar must have applied to the church of Emly, which claimed seniority in Munster in this period. The legal tracts of the period give as exemplars of 'great church settlements' Emly and Cork and there is further evidence to suggest that these three churches, Emly, Lismore and Cork, may have exercised some kind of metropolitan or archepisco-pal authority in Desmuma as a whole over a patchwork of other *paruchiae*. Only these three churches alone in this territory are served with a near complete annalistic record of leadership succession while it must be no coincidence that the usurper, Brian Boru, when investing Desmuma upon his taking of the kingship of Munster as a whole, in 987, exercised his lordship over the entire ecclesiastical establishment of Desmuma by a hostage taking hosting to the churches of Cork, Emly and Lismore.[29] There were of course other powerful church centres here, such as Scattery, Cloyne, Ardfert and Rosscarbery, whose annalistic record, while not com-plete, is still significant (see Appendix A). As we have seen above Ardfert may have been subservient to Lismore and it seems certain that, at least for periods, Rosscarbery was subject to Cork.[30]

Turning to the question of Cloyne's place in such a putative schema, we must once again turn to its chief lay patrons, Síl Cathail/Eóganacht Glennamnach, for the clue which will lead to illumination. Cloyne was not the only ecclesiastical benefactor of this lineage, whose attachment to and association with Emly is attested in annals of the eighth century.[31] That this association persisted long after is suggested by the name of a prominent member of the lineage in Desmuma, Giolla Ailbi Ua Caoimh,

---

27 Etchingham 1993, 139; 1994, 49. **28** Ibid., 122–4. **29** Ibid., 162–3, 181, 214; *AI* 987.2. **30** Ó Corráin 1985a. **31** *AI, A Tig,* 742; *A Clon* 790; *AU* 792 (= 793).

in 1194, Ailbe being, of course, the patron saint of Emly.[32] As we shall see presently, there is reason to believe that Cloyne was subject to some kind of ecclesiastical overlordship by Emly, at least during the eleventh and early twelfth centuries, and it seems to me that all of this shows a triple linkage between both churches and this royal lineage. After a hiatus of nearly two centuries the annalistic record for Cloyne recommences with the obit of Mac Geláin, *airchinnech* of Cluain Uama, in 1060.[33] This is followed by that of another *airchinnech*, Ua Carráin, in 1092, and then the death of its abbot, Mael Muad Mac Meic Clothna, of plague, three years later. This Mael Muad was the grandson of Clothna Muimnech, an abbot of Emly who died in 1048, and whose descendants, the Uí Chlothna, remained of importance in Emly until the Anglo-Norman invasion and provided a thirteenth-century bishop of Ross, Finghín (Florentius). Other ecclesiastical families associated with Emly (and genealogically derived from local groups with ancient associations with Emly) were the Uí Laígenáin and Uí Dubchróin. In 1159 Bishop Ua Dubchróin, abbot of Cloyne, died, as did Diarmait Ua Laígenáin, *fer léginn* of Cloyne, three years later. Significantly, Ua Laígenáin was slain by Ua Ciarmhaic, king of Eóganacht Áine, the territory in which Emly lay. Yet another Emly surname associated with a clerical presence in Cloyne is Ua Lígdae and Ó Buachalla has suggested that the well-established presence of three other surnames originating in the Emly area in and around Cloyne in the thirteenth and fourteenth centuries can be attributed to associations between both churches in the pre-invasion period.[34]

Therefore the earliest identifiable connexions between Cloyne and another major monastery lie with Emly, and begin at least before the end of the eleventh century. The full extent of this connexion is denied us by the poor state of the annalistic record for Cloyne at this period. This linkage may be much older but lack of evidence precludes any certainty here. No such reciprocal settlement of Cloyne families is noted at

---

32 *MIA* 1194.5. 33 All annalistic references to church heads of Cloyne are given in 9.3 below. 34 Byrne 1984, 253; Ó Corráin 1980, 164; Ó Buachalla 1945b, 84–5; *AI* 995.5, 1028.7, 1052.5, 1058.4, 1122.3, 1163.5; *AU* 1058.

Emly, suggesting that in this relationship Emly was dominant. From this it would appear that Cloyne was in some way subject to an ecclesiastical overlordship exercised by Emly, which may have been in existence since at least 987, when no mention of Cloyne occurs in the list of those senior-churches of Desmuma placed under his authority by Brian Boru in that year. Emly's position near the seat of power in Munster, Cashel, made it an especially important church and, as we have already noted, it claimed pre-eminence in Munster. From this it would seem that the *paruchia* of Cloyne may have been, at various stages, subject to an super-paruchial or archiepiscopal type ecclesiastical lordship exercised by Emly. We have already seen how the dominant lay power in both Cloyne and Emly in the period until the mid-ninth century was Síl Cathail and this leads to the inevitable suspicion that the association between these churches must have its origins no later than the fall from provincial kingship of the latter power during the ninth century.

8.6 Ailbe and Mac Léinín

One further possibility here is that this relationship between churches may have something to do with the origins of Colmán Mac Léinín. I have already demonstrated (3.1, 3.2) how the early genealogies of Mac Léinín derive him from a branch of the Cattraige people settled immediately to the north of Emly. The history of the church of Emly (Imblech Ibair) and of its founder, Ailbe, is typically shrouded in later traditions which obscure the fact that little is known for certain about either. The eighth century traditions promoted by Emly concerning its founder located him in time in the late fifth–early sixth centuries.[35] If these traditions are correct then Emly was already a leading church during the *floruit* of Mac Léinín. It is not unreasonable to suppose that our saint and his family were members of the ecclesiastical community of Emly at some level or other during his early years and/or young adulthood. Did

---

35 *CS* 532; *AU* 534, 542; *AFM* 541; Plummer 1910, 47–64; Ryan 118.

he take this probable early connexion with him to Cloyne and establish some kind of relationship between his ancestral church and his new foundation? Yet another link between Emly/Ailbe and Mac Léinín exists. We have already seen how it seems probable that a seventh century source identifies Mac Léinín's branch of the Cattraige as an hereditary clerical family with Emly associations, and that one genealogical schema links the Cattraige with the Araid, another early people, several branches of whom occupied the general Limerick/Tipperary border area (3.2). The genealogies of the Araid derive Ailbe from this people, as does his earlier pedigree in the *Corpus*.[36] Therefore it would appear that Ailbe of Emly – if indeed his origins are correctly given – and Colmán Mac Léinín belonged to two closely related peoples occupying the same territory.

This in turn leads us to consideration of the phenomenon of claimed or pretended descent from the founding saint of a church by its later hereditary clerical lineage. In the case of Cloyne the early disappearance of the Cattraige from the historical record – they are not listed among those communities with Emly connexions in the late-ninth century *Vita Tripartita* – renders this question insoluble. Turning to the same question in relation to Emly, note that most of its leaders with identifiable pedigrees are connected to various branches of the Eóganacht.[37] Some of their related peoples, however, were somewhat more enduring in the land than the Cattraige. Annalistic records show some of these still as local powers until at least the eleventh century.[38] Ó Riain has identified leaders of the church of Emly who died in 781 and 1074 with men who occur in the Daulrige/Dál Modula pedigree of the late eleventh century.[39]

8.7 Emly: senior church of Munster

In light of the above relationship between Cloyne and Emly it may be that something of the hidden history of Cloyne's fortunes before the late eleventh century can be discerned in those of Emly. The central role

36 Ó Raithbheartaigh 139; *CGH* p. 386; *CSH* 135. **37** Stokes 1887, 202; Ó Riain 1997b, 707; Byrne 1984, 252–3. **38** *AI* 1045.14. **39** Ó Riain 2002, 293n; *CGH* p. 387.

played by the latter church in the ecclesiastical and political affairs of Munster, which was so clearly evident during the eighth century in tandem with that of Síl Cathail, did not cease with the decline of the latter dynasty. Throughout the ninth century the leadership of the church of Emly was dominated by a family of local origin, derived from Eóganacht Áine. One of these leaders was Cenn Fáelad Ua Mugthigirn, leader of the church of Emly in the period 858–72 and also king of Munster for most of the same period (859–72). A few years earlier Ólchobar Mac Cináeda had also filled both roles simultaneously, in the period 847–51. His lineage is confused but he may also have been of the Eóganacht Áine.[40] From this it will be seen that Emly remained close to the centre of political power in Munster from the period of the earliest records down to the late ninth century, during much the same period in which it seems to have exercised some real or claimed ecclesiastical jurisdiction over much of Munster. During the century after 872 political power in Munster passed mostly into the hands of those segments of Eóganacht Chaisil who now came to monopolize the style after the fall from power of Síl Cathail, and whose demesne territories probably lay around Cashel itself. That Emly likely remained the chief church of these rulers is suggested by the 930 slaying of its abbot by an unspecified group of 'Eóganacht'.[41] After the death of Donnchad, last Eóganacht Chaisil king of Munster, in 963, the long-established privileged position of Emly finally came under threat from the new usurping Dál Cais dynasty in the shape of Mathgamain mac Cennétig and later his brother, Brian Boru. The first sign of this change is recorded in 968, when Mathgamain raided Eóganacht Áine and plundered Emly. Five years later, and now king of Munster, Mathgamain imposed a settlement in an ecclesiastical dispute between Emly and Armagh in favour of the latter, the first sign of the continuing Dál Cais preference for Armagh over the older Munster ecclesiastical establishment. This dispute seems to have centered on Emly's resistance to Armagh's claims of ecclesiastical primacy.[42]

---

40 Byrne 1984, 252; Ó Corráin 1980, 164. **41** *A Clon* p. 150. **42** *AI* 968, 973.6. For a remarkable Dál Cais expression of hatred of Emly, see Ó Corráin 1981b, 229–30.

Mathgamain's brother Brian, upon his consolidation of power in Munster after the former's death, soon imposed his overlordship by force on Emly and the other major churches of Desmuma. This was shortly followed by his removal of the sitting abbot and imposition of his own candidate here, an event which occurred in 986.[43] That such a tactic was at that time confined to Emly is strongly suggestive of the power and substance of this church, with its ancient Eóganacht associations, and the threat it must have posed to the new Dál Cais rulers. Brian Boru appears to have had sound reason for such a move, as subsequent events would show. After his death his sons feuded and the Eóganacht Chaisil were able to regain some measure of independence and power, at least in *Aurmuma*. Their kings, however, the Uí Donnchada, were not descended from the last pre-Dalcassian Eóganacht Chaisil king, Donnchad, who had died in 963, but from an earlier king, Máel Fathartaig (+ 957), of a rival line.[44] The survival of Donnchad's line, in the person of his son, Sáerbrethach, was assured by the acquisition of the coarbial rulership of the great church of Emly, probably after Boru's death.[45] Thus once again Emly would play a pivotal role in the politics of Munster by providing a political platform for a lineage which would spawn the later Meic Carthaig kings whose power would rival that of Boru's own descendants, the Uí Briain. After Sáerbrethach's death, in 1025, Emly seems to have continued to pursue an anti-Dalcassian policy, if the defensive slaying of a Dál Cais dynast by its *muinter* in 1032 is anything to go by.[46] Meanwhile Sáerbrethach's son, Carthach, had finally triumphed over the Uí Donnchada in the battle for the kingship of Eóganacht Chaisil. Carthach was in turn succeeded by his son, Muiredach ('mac Carthaig'), who seized the leadership of Emly in 1052 by deposing an apparently pro-Dalcassian abbot. No doubt using his position at Emly as a powerbase, Muiredach went on to become king of Eóganacht Chaisil in turn (1057–92).[47] For much of the eleventh century this kingdom, in alliance with their eastern neighbours, Ossrige, maintained virtual independence from Uí Briain overlordship.

---

43 *AI* 986.3. **44** *AI* 1027.4, 1039.6, 1052.3, 1057.2; Kelleher, 240–1. **45** Byrne 1984, 253. **46** *AI* 1032.9. **47** *AI* 1045.8, 1052.5, 1054.7, 1092.7.

This period of relative independence for Eóganacht Chaisil was brought to a close by the end of a period of weak Uí Briain kings in Munster with the advent firstly of Tairdelbach Ua Briain (1072–86) and then of his son, Muirchertach (1086–1119). These powerful kings, whose sway came to extend over much of Ireland, needed a compliant Munster as a base and the rival threat posed by an independent Eóganacht Chaisil was intolerable. Accordingly this was eliminated, probably by the banishment of the senior nobles of Eóganacht Chaisil from their homeland southwards towards the Cork area around the turn of the twelfth century, in turn probably facilitated by the factional in-fighting which followed the death of Muiredach mac Carthaig. Muirchertach Ua Briain is best remembered as the sponsor of major ecclesiastical reform in Ireland, especially by his promotion of the synod of Cashel in 1101, and that of Ráith Breasail in 1111, at which the later diocesan structure of the Irish Church was born. At the council of Cashel Muirchertach donated Cashel itself to the church, thus depriving his chief local rivals, the now banished Eóganacht Chaisil, of their ancient stronghold, and at Ráith Breasail, no doubt again under Muirchertach's influence, the ancient claims to supremacy in Munster by Emly were put aside in favour of the new archbishopric of Cashel. Thus Ua Briain eliminated both his local political rivals and their chief church and ecclesiastical power-base. What of Cloyne in all of this? The annalistic record for eleventh-century Desmuma is particularly sparse but the links between Cloyne and Emly already noted suggest where we might generally place Cloyne and its *paruchia*. It is a reasonable speculation to suggest that the Eóganacht Glennamnach must have been closer to the Eóganacht Chaisil cause than to that of the usurper Dál Cais and we may also speculate that Cloyne, influenced both by the leading secular power in its *paruchia* and its links with Emly, must have maintained a similar position. There is, in fact, some evidence to render the latter more than mere speculation. Having banished (or being about to do so) the Eóganacht Chaisil southwards to around Cork, Muirchertach could hardly leave them to their own devices, which must account in part for the arrival of the first of four Dalcassian placements in the leadership of the church of Cork, in

1085. Another suspect church with Eóganacht sympathies must have been Cloyne, to judge by the plundering of both it and Cork three years later by Diarmait, brother of Muirchertach.[48] Furthermore, as Ó Buachalla[49] has long ago noted, the presence in the Cloyne area of surnames – some actually associated with the church of Cloyne and its lands – of undoubted Dalcassian origin in the period from the late twelfth to the early fourteenth century suggests a period of dominance of Cloyne by the Uí Briain, as has already been noted in relation to the churches of Emly and Cork, probably during the lifetime of Muirchertach Ua Briain. All of which finally leads to consideration of the question of the origins of the present diocese of Cloyne and its relationship to what had gone before.

48 Ó Corráin 1985a; *AI* 1088.2.　**49** Ó Buachalla 1945b, 85–86.

CHAPTER NINE

The diocese of Cloyne

Contrary to the belief of historians of the 'Old-School', the process of diocesan formation in Ireland was not a new departure in the early twelfth century but would seem to have had its roots in, and been derived from, the older paruchial system. In order to fully understand this process we need to take cognisance of recent advances in our understanding of church history in the centuries before the twelfth-century reforms. The nature of the *paruchia*, the system of leadership practised in the *paruchia*, and the similarity between *paruchia* and the then foreign term diocese must be teased out before going on to treat of the specific question of the origins of the diocese of Cloyne.

9.1 Paruchia *and diocese*

The principal eighth-century collection of Irish canon law (*Collectio Canonum Hibernensis*), indicates that at that time a *paruchia* was primarily conceived of as a bishop's sphere of pastoral jurisdiction, which, furthermore, was represented as being clearly demarcated and geographically cohesive. Far from this situation deteriorating towards a system of dispersed monastic filiation in the centuries that followed, as has sometimes been suggested, evidence from the annals and from hagiography clearly illustrates that this paruchial system remained the norm until the period of the twelfth century reforms.[1]

9.2 Church government

The paruchial system of ecclesiastical organization in existence at this

---

1 Etchingham 1994, 62; 1999, 12–20, 106–114; Sharpe 1992, 86.

period in Ireland has been summarized as embracing 'episcopacy, abbacy and 'coarbial' authority within a single, flexible system of ecclesiastical headship', and again, as 'a single, eclectic structure embracing episcopal, abbatial and temporal authority in a variety of possible permutations'.[2] Three classes of such ecclesiastical headship are found in this system, that of abbot, bishop and *airchinnech*.

The term abbot (*abb, abbas*) on the surface indicates conventional cenobitic monastic leadership. As the term is found in the canons, hagiography and annals of the period under study, however, it seems to be used in a much looser or terminologically flexible sense to indicate simple headship, and should not be understood as always or even often referring to the conventional image. While conventional monastic forms of organization may indeed have existed throughout this period the terminology of monasticism, especially that of abbot, was appropriated for use in many, non-cenobitic situations. As occurring in the sources the use of the term abbot has been described as 'ambiguous and often denotes monastic or spiritual leadership, but is also frequently treated as a synonym of *comarbae* and *airchinnech* to designate the lord of the church and of its dependants'. This process was even more marked in Celtic Scotland.[3] In much the same way as the term 'abbot' outgrew its strictly monastic meaning, so too did the other key terms of monastic origin associated with the Early Irish Church, *manach* and *mainistir*. The semantic range of the former ran from monk to lay tenant of ecclesiastical land.[4] The latter term derives, of course, from the latin *monasterium* 'monastery'. The same etymology in Anglo-Saxon England gave the term 'minster'. There evidence of actual church organization in the eighth–tenth-century period is significantly more abundant than in Ireland and gives a clear picture of pastoral care exercised through large 'parishes' served by teams of priests and other clergy, some of whom may have been monks under vows, operating from important central churches familiarly called minsters, the areas of which were usually termed

2 Ibid., 47, 104–5. **3** Ibid., 55–8, 80–3, 99–100. Mr Kenneth Nicholls informs me that in Scotland *ab* was used instead of *comharba* of purely lay heads of ecclesiastical establishments such as Abernethy and Dunkeld. **4** Ibid., 363–453.

parochiae or minster parishes. Sharpe has suggested, certainly with justification, that this organizational model is much more likely to represent something like the model of the Irish Church of the same period than the 'Celtic Monastic' model with its contorted, unauthentic and historically unsound basis.[5]

The Irish term *airchinnech* 'ecclesiastical head' (corresponding to the Latin *princeps*) again shows terminological flexibility in its usage. It features both as a general term for church leadership where the actual leadership role could be held by either a bishop or abbot, and more specifically as a non-clerical ruler charged with governance of the temporalities and dependant population of his church, where the episcopal function would appear to have existed also but at an inferior or perhaps collegial level. High moral standards were, however, expected of such a lay head, suggesting perhaps some degree of minor orders.[6] A related term is *comarbae* 'successor'. In the canons this simply offers yet another alternative term for *princeps* and the title, at least in the earlier period, has no specifically lay connotations.[7]

In the case of bishops, the canons indicate that this title carried the conventional meaning of pastoral authority. As with the other terms discussed above, a marked degree of terminological flexibility is again noted in the sources. In the vernacular legal material the bishop is rarely portrayed as handling temporalities and is usually portrayed as a dignitary of high legal and social status, indispensible to his church's own standing and who may perform a key judicial function. Etchingham concludes that (in relation to the same sources) 'the bishop and *airchinnech* and the functions they represent are not treated as alternatives, still less as rival sources of authority, but as complementary, since the presence of both are characteristics of the church which is in good order and of high status'. As against this a study of the annals for the period indicates that 'after about AD 750, the option of combining episcopal rank with effective headship of a church continued to be exercised and was by no means redundant or even unusual'.[8]

---

5 Ibid., 111–13; Sharpe 1992, passim. 6 Etchingham 1999, 45, 64, 72–4, 78–9. 7 Ibid., 67–8, 71–3. 8 Ibid., 47–83, 99–104.

In summary then, the level of terminological flexibility evident in the usage of Irish church governance during this period renders difficult the interpretation of the annalistic material in relation to individual churches and suggests a need for caution in how such evidence is interpreted. While the term 'bishop' is unambiguious, the terms 'abbot', *airchinnech* and *comarbae* could be interchangeable while the latter could be used in all contexts of church headship. Finally the term *airchinnech* also carried a specific meaning of non-clerical church head, although with standards of moral rectitude attached which suggested a paraclerical state. A further problem relates to the nature of the annalistic evidence for such titles. Our principal sources for the personnel of church governance are the annals and it would appear that the redactors of two of our major sources, the *Annals of the Four Masters* and the *Annals of Inisfallen*, had a tendency to substitute the term 'abbot' for other terms as part of a general process of redaction, thus distorting the record by exaggerating the importance of this term.[9]

Turning to the question of actual episcopal authority, an eighth-century prescription, *Ríagal Phátraic*, suggests that by then bishops had established an extensive control over small foundations, whatever their origins, secular or monastic.[10] Etchingham's study of the sources reveals an interesting situation. These sources, in particular the annals, contain much more Leinster and Meath material than from other areas of Ireland but there is no reason to suggest that the reality of church governance was any different in these parts of Ireland then in the remainder. The evidence clearly points to a number of startling conclusions. Both the canons and hagiography suggest that mimimal polities, such as the *tuath* in its original sense, could constitute the basic sphere of episcopal jurisdiction. Even more startling is the evidence for a territorial episcopal hierarchy drawn from canon and vernacular law, hagiography and the annals.[11] As regards the latter source, Etchingham is best left speak for himself. 'The series of tenth century episcopal titles [in the annals] is

---

9 Ibid., 97–9, 101–4. **10** Sharpe 1992, 101. **11** Etchingham 1999, 70–1, 133–5, 149–71, 177–94; Charles-Edwards, 65–6, 71–2; Ó Corráin 1994, 30–1; Sharpe 1992, 106.

compelling evidence for real spheres of authority and tiers of jurisdiction. These, as far as one can tell, were not characterized by long-term stability, but tended to fluctuate, in which respect they may have reflected the secular political scene. The other annalistic evidence adduced here is consistent with a model of relatively numerous small local bishoprics, the locations and dimensions of which may also have been subject to the ebb and flow of ecclesiastical and, it may be suspected, secular politics.'[11a] We must next turn to the application of this picture of organization to the evidence for our area of study.

9.3 Church government in Cloyne

Before proceeding it will be best to reproduce the actual annalistic and other entries of relevance.

*c.*697 *Eochaid, abb Clúanae Húamae* [attestation] (*Cáin Adomnáin*).

821 *Cucaech abb Cluana hUamha, dég* (*AFM*).

859 *Maelcoba óa Faelan abbas Cluana Uamha* [obituary] (*AU*, 858 = 859, and *AFM*, 857).

871 *Quies Neill m. Donngaile, abb Cluana Huama 7 Cuile Collaingge* (*AI*).

884 *Reachtaidh, suí-epscop Cluana hUamhach* [obituary] (*AFM*).

885 *Feargal mac Finachta, epscop agus abb Cluana hUamha 7 hUamanán mac Cérén, secnap Cluana hUamha, do marbhadh le Nortmannaibh* (*AFM*, better in *Cogadh Gaedhel re Gallaibh*).[11b]

1060 *Mac Gelain, airchinnech Cluana Huama, quieuit* (*AI*).

1092 *Hua Carráin, airchinnech Cluana Húama, quieuit in Christo* (*AI*).

11a Etchingham 1999, 194. **11**b Todd 1867, 28. Both *Cogadh* and *AFM* must have been quoting from a common annalistic source for this reference, only the former giving the full reference. For a useful discussion of annalistic material in *Cogadh* see Ní Mhaonaigh, 122–3.

1095   *Moel Muad mc. meic Clothnai, abb Cluana Huma* [obituary] (*AI*).

1099   *Uamhnachan Ua Meictire, comarba Mic Leinin* [obituary] (*AU, AFM*)

1149   *Giolla na Naomh Ua Muircheartaigh, uasalescop deiscirt Erenn, seanoir ogh eccnaidhe cráibhdheach* [obituary] (*AFM*).

1159   *In t-epscop Ua Dubcroin, ab Cluana Uama, quieuit in Christo* (*AI*).

1162   *Dondchad Ua Cineada quieuit in Christo in Cluain Uama* (*AI*).

1162   *Diarmaid Ua Laighnen, fear leighinn Cluana hUamha, saoi Mumhan, marbhadh lá hUibh Ciarmhaic* (*AFM*).

1167   *In t-espoc Ua Flandacan .i. espoc Cluana hUama, quieuit in Christo* (*A. Tig.*; in error in *AFM*).

This evidence can be broken into two sections divided by the *lacuna* between 885 and 1060. It is probable that Cloyne originated as an actual cenobitic monastery, but it is unclear to what extent, if any, this element subsequently came to play in the history of the church there. It might be suggested that abbot Eochaid represents an authentic monastic abbot but no such confidence can be felt regarding the ninth century annals. Of the four abbots noted in this century the sole authority for one is *AFM* while that for another is *AI*. The former source in particular has been shown to be untrustworthy as a seventeenth-century transmitter of its older exemplars due to an editorial policy of altering diverse titular leadership terminology to standard forms and thus obscuring the original terms. Thus we have no way of knowing what the actual title born by Cúcaéch was, while there must also be some doubt in the case of Niall mac Donngaile. Only in the case of Maelcoba (859) and Feargal mac Fínachta (885) can we be sure that the actual title was abbot, the former given the generally reliable nature of the *Annals of Ulster* in such matters. As to the latter, the reference of 885 from *AFM* survives in much earlier and fuller form in the early twelfth-century *Cogadh Gaedhel re Gallaibh,* which shows that Feargal was bishop as well as abbot of Cloyne, and even here the title is at least as likely to be used in the sense of general church head as distinct from monastic superior. The mention of a prior of Cloyne in 885 is merely a seventeenth-century alteration as *Cogadh* shows the original term used here was *secnap*, a term often translated as prior but better as vice-abbot or deputy-head, again a term with a broad range of meaning and not at all what it might seem at first sight.

The second period brings somewhat more clarity. The title *airchinnech* as used in the obituaries of 1060 and 1092 almost certainly refers to non-clerical headship. Airchinnech Ua Carráin is the first recorded member of a local regnal family, apparently of Uí Meic Caille origins, who may have used his headship to secure local political power as well, although given my earlier comments regarding the political importance of the church of Cloyne (8.3) one wonders if his political position was at least equal, if not greater, than that of the local *rí* (if indeed the positions were not sometimes jointly held).[12] Ua Carráin's death was shortly followed by that of an 'abbot' with close Emly associations (8.5). Was Mael Muad the representative of an Emly interest in competition with local polities for leadership of Cloyne? I have already suggested (8.6) that the Emly connexion with Cloyne may be very ancient and its interest in Cloyne may have been of a metropolitian or hierarchical nature. Were these interests possibly being promoted by the Eóganacht Glennamnach or/and Eóganacht Chaisil at a time of great dispute between the latter and the dominant Uí Briain in Munster? Perhaps the certainly diminished distinction between these titles by that time merely indicated that the same position of headship was in contest between an abbot and an *airchinnech* representing rival interests, local *versus* regional. Whatever of this yet another power in the area must have subsequently succeeded to the headship as suggested by the obituary of *Comarba* Ua Meic Tíre. This sept seems to represent a rival and more distantly related line of the local Uí Liatháin grouping – of which the Uí Meic Caille were the main segment – and once again and in time-honoured fashion appear to have used the headship of this powerful church as a stepping stone to local

12 Ó Corráin 1979, 173–6.

power.[13] These families continued to vie for local lordship into the next century. In 1151 Gilla Gott Ua Carráin, lord or king of Uí Meic Caille, was slain at Coole by the Uí Meic Tíre.[14] This incident must have had some connexion with Cloyne as Coole was an ecclesiastical dependency; was Ua Carráin also *airchinnech* of Cloyne? Yet another local family with connexions to the headship of Cloyne were the Uí Cineada. One of this family was described as *rígdamna* of Uí Liatháin in his obituary of 1127. The 1162 obituary of Donnchad Ua Cinaeda, while not naming him as head of Cloyne, strongly implies as much. These are the only sept native to the Cloyne area to have associations with another major church. The annals record the death of *Airchinnech* Dub Dá Leithe Ua Cinaeda of Cork, in 1057.[15] The remaining entries above indicate both a Lismore connexion and further Emly connexions with Cloyne and these will be dealt with below.

9.4 The see of Cloyne before AD 1100

I have already cited the evidence adduced by Etchingham and Sharpe for the existence of territorial episcopacy and archiepiscopacy in Ireland long before the twelfth century and its 'reforms'. One of the problems with applying this evidence in a south Munster context is the sparse nature of the annalistic record. This is summarized in Appendix A. This tabulation of the evidence reveals several interesting features. Only in the case of Emly, Lismore and Cork is the annalistic record of church headship complete or nearly so and I have already suggested (8.4) that these great churches represented a tier of ecclesiastical super-authority in south Munster, with perhaps in turn Emly as supreme. Sharpe goes so far as to suggest a four tiered level of church hierarchy in the period before AD 1000, with local or district churches subject to a bishop of the *tuath* or minimal polity, he in turn subject to a bishop seated in a major church centre with its extensive *paruchia*, and he in turn subject to the

---

13 Ó Murchadha; Ó Buachalla 1939, 33–5; *PRC* 229, note 257. 14 *AFM.* 15 *AFM* 1057; *AI* 1127.13; Ó Corráin 1985a; Ó Buachalla 1939, 28; 1945a, 26.

bishop seated in the senior church of his province.[16] A study of the material in Appendix A suggests that, in applying this possible schema to south Munster, we should posit a pyramid with Emly at the apex, under which would be Cork and Lismore, in turn over Cloyne, Rosscarbery, Scattery and Ardfert, each in turn over a collection of local bishops of minimal polities. The evidence adduced above even suggests the direct 'line-management' structure of such a schema, as we have noted evidence that Emly was senior to Cloyne, Lismore to Ardfert and perhaps Scattery, and Cork to Rosscarbery. Note the existence of pre-1100 bishops in all of these churches. Indeed within the area in which these churches are found there appears to be no annalistic record of bishops in any other centre, making a very strong argument indeed for a significant level of continuity between the so-called 'reformed' period and what had gone before. To return to Appendix A, the increasingly sparse nature of the record as we move south-westwards must reflect *lacunae* in the annalistic record.

The question might well be asked, what of evidence for the lowest tier of episcopacy, the bishops of each minimal polity (*epscop túaithe*)? The area of best annalistic coverage is Meath, and here Etchingham has found some evidence for just such a tier of bishops, whose sees would later act as template for the rural deaneries established in the early thirteenth century.[17] While there is no evidence for a similar origin for the later ruri-decanal structure in Cloyne this may simply be due to gaps in the historical record. It will be remembered that the chief complaint of the foreign promoters of the later reforms, Lanfranc and Anselm, was not an insufficiency but an excessive multiplicity of bishops in the Ireland of the late eleventh century. (Lanfranc speaks of 'many bishops ordained in towns and cities', a charge perhaps to be understood in terms of bishops of minimal polities.)[18] It may be that such *epscoip túaithe* were so numerous and commonplace in the social scale that they are noticed only where annalistic coverage is most extensive. If this were the case it would

16 Sharpe 1992, 106; Etchingham 1999, 153–5. **17** Etchingham 1999, 179, 192–3; Wilkins, 547. **18** Watt, 6–7.

certainly explain the lack of such references from south Munster, where even the episcopal record for the major churches is meagre indeed. Another pertinent insight here may be that of Ó Corráin, who has drawn attention to the eighth-century Gaulish phenomenon of the *chorepiscopus*, who did not dwell in a cathedral city and lacked full episcopal dignity, and identified these with the Irish *conepiscopi* of the canons, whose role seems close to that of the *epscop túaithe*.[19] To an extent however, this discussion is irrelevant in a south Munster context. While the evidence for this suggested tier of *epscoip túaithe* is lacking here the same cannot be said to be the case with the putative next tier up in the hierarchy, that of bishops attached to major church centres, as I have illustrated above.

To turn from the general to the specific, annalistic and other references give us the names of two early bishops of Cloyne, *suí-epscop* Rechtaid who died in 884 and Fergal mac Fínachta, *epscop agus abb Cluana hUamha,* slain by Norse raiders in 885. Feargal followed a common pattern of the period by holding both the abbacy and episcopacy of Cloyne, although the former is probably to be understood in the sense of general church head or administrator of the temporalities, rather than monastic superior, as indicated above in my discussion of monastic terminology as used in this period in Ireland. What of *suí-epscop* Rechtaid of Cloyne, who died in 884? Etchingham draws attention to the significance of this term and offers a range of meanings: 'learned bishop', 'pre-eminent bishop', 'supreme among bishops', and goes on to suggest the sense of a bishop 'appointed to a position of especial dignity and authority', an argument supported by the locations attached to such titled bishops, almost all of which later became the seats of 'reformed' bishoprics.[20] In a south Munster context it is interesting to note that the term is also used of bishops of Emly and Rosscarbery.[21] I would suggest that this term might indicate that Rechtaid of Cloyne was bishop of the *paruchia* of Cloyne, which may already have been very extensive, as I have suggested above (8.3; 8.4). In light of this discussion I would also suggest that he was merely one of a line of regular bishops of Cloyne,

---

19 Ó Corráin 1987, 306; 1994, 31. **20** Etchingham 1999, 182–5. **21** *AFM* 979, 1085.

originating perhaps centuries earlier, and which continued down to the time of the later 'reforms'. That Rechtaid appears to have been immediately succeeded as bishop of Cloyne by Fergal mac Fínachta is surely highly significant in this context. That only these two among their many putative colleagues has found remembrance in the written record is, I would suggest, more a reflection on the failings of that same record than on those of the episcopacy of Cloyne. The very importance and power of the ancient church of Cloyne, as illustrated above, is further mute testament to the likelihood of this scenario, for how could such a major church centre operate without a bishop from whom all pastoral care must flow? To quote Ignatius of Antioch, writing in AD 110, 'Where the bishop is present, there let the congregation gather, just as where Jesus Christ is, there is the Catholic Church.'[22]

In summary then, I would suggest that the great church of Cloyne, like its fellows, had been born of a cenobitic urge, the success of which soon drew others to it and saw it over time become a worldly power. Over the centuries this church, sponsored by a great dynasty, grew in power and wealth, a wealth reflected in its impressive streets and religious monuments. Staffed by numerous clergy, some of whom may have been monks under vows, and other hereditary clergy, more canons than monks, all under the presiding authority of an important bishop, Cloyne must have operated both a school of law and higher learning and a seminary where the *maccléirech* or clerical student was prepared for pastoral duties within its broad *paruchia*. Meanwhile its temporal affairs were administered both by powerful local lords and those drawn from its superior church of Emly. While the actual process of growth of its *paruchia* is difficult to measure precisely, the extent of the latter, by the late eleventh century, is likely to have approximated to the area of the 'reformed' diocese.[23] This is suggested by the extensive area of distribution of the cult of Colmán mac Léinín and associated cults, all of which can hardly have sprung up overnight after the birth of the 'reformed'

22 As quoted by Schreck, 58. **23** Liam Ó Buachalla was moving in the same direction towards the end of his all too-short life and, had he lived longer, would, I believe, have certainly reached a similar conclusion. (Gwynn 234–5.)

diocese and must certainly have been in existence before the synod of Ráith Breasail in 1111, at which the *paruchia* of Cloyne was carved up and expropriated by unsympathetic interests.

9.5 The 'reformed' see of Cloyne

I have already treated of the political situation in south Munster during the eleventh century (8.6). To recap briefly, the major regional political dynamic of that century was the continued effort of the Uí Briain to maintain political dominance in Munster in the face of rebellion by the heirs of the older regnal tradition, the Eóganacht Chaisil. Given the close relationship between church and secular politics in the society of the time an ecclesiastical dimension to this struggle was unavoidable. While Muircheartach Ua Briain is rightly remembered as the greatest native sponsor of ecclesiastical reform the political realities of his period made inevitable some element of political self-serving by Ua Briain here. This is especially obvious in two aspects of the reforms. In his own family's immediate sphere of interest the new 'reformed' dioceses of Killaloe and Limerick had swallowed up a number of older mother-churches, several of which had long records of opposition to Dalcassian interference.[24] Secondly, his donation to the church of what must have been the recently won swordland of Cashel and his promotion of that see to metropolitan status in place of the older Eóganacht chief mother-church of Emly, thus 'killing two birds with one stone'. There are, however, several other indications of this self-serving in the reforms, not least in the treatment of the church of Cloyne.

The territory of the new dioceses of Killaloe, Limerick, Cashel and Emly[25] were either part of the Dalcassian home territory or had experienced settlements by Dalcassian elements as part of the expansion of the latter power, and so were safely within the immediate Uí Briain sphere

---

24 Ó Corráin 1973, 53–7. **25** That this was so in the case of Emly is suggested by the presence of an Uí Briain fortress at Dún Trí Liag and the death of Brian Boru's daughter at Emly. *AFM* 1054; *AU* 1080.

of influence. The creation of the large diocese of Ratass or Iarmuma may perhaps be seen as a reward for the continued loyalty to Dalcassian power of the ruling family of Ciarraige, Uí Chonchobair, the diocesan seat of which lay within their territory. Turning to the diocese of Lismore, something similar appears to have been the case, given the Uí Bric loyalty to the Dalcassian interest.[26] Indeed such was the esteem in which this church was held by Muircheartach that, upon his fall from political power, he retired there. It must also be significant that no similar Dalcassian takeover of leadership as had occurred in several other major churches in Munster is noted in relation to Lismore. This left only the Co. Cork churches to deal with. It was this very area to which the defeated nobles of Eóganacht Chaisil appear to have forged a new power-base early in the twelfth century, while, even outside of this, the churches of Cork and Cloyne had represented a sufficient threat to Muircheartach's interests to require the insertion of Dalcassian placemen therein. Even apart from the newly arrived Eóganacht Chaisil, the presence of the older native Eóganacht groupings in the area, such as Glennamnach and Uí Echach, represented a significant potential threat to the Uí Briain and required the ecclesiastical 'pacification' of the area. I would suggest that the form of the diocesan structure here after Ráith Breasail owes much to these considerations. Cork was too important a centre to have its *paruchia* dismembered and this was actually supplemented by the addition of what was probably the *paruchia* of Rosscarbery and a portion of that of Cloyne (Múscraige Mitíne), so that the new diocese of Cork came to comprise everything west of Cork Harbour and south of the Blackwater.[27] Uí Briain control of this important diocese was ensured by the continued presence of Dalcassian placemen in its bishopric.[28]

What is most startling is Ráith Breasail's treatment of the *paruchia* of Cloyne, which was entirely dismembered. Uí Meic Caille and Cloyne itself went to Lismore, while Fir Maige and Múscraige Ua nDonnagáin went to Emly, reflecting perhaps some partial recognition of the old claim to overlordship of the church of Cloyne by the latter, while in the

26 Jefferies, 83–5. **27** MacErlean, 3–4. **28** Ó Corráin 1985a.

process locking in the Uí Chaím/ Eóganacht Glennamnach heartland to an ecclesiastical dominance by an area which had featured significant recent Uí Briain settlement (6.2). The sundering of the ecclesiastical link between the neighbouring Múscraige kingdoms is particularly striking in view of the evidence of long-existing shared political and ecclesiastical connexions between both related polities.[29] We have already seen (8.7) how Muircheartach Ua Briain had probably inserted placemen in Cloyne some decades earlier and the obvious odium in which this church was held by the Dalcassian interest must be principally explained by its long associations with both the Eóganacht Glennamnach polity and the church of Emly and the threat posed by polity and church to Dalcassian dominance of Munster.

What happened next is unclear in detail but clear in broad outline, and continues to owe much to the contemporary political climate in Munster. It is usually assumed that the 'reformed' diocese of Cloyne was created as the synod of Kells-Mellifont in 1152. This assumption, however, does not accord with the evidence. In Bernard of Clairvaux's life of the leading reformer, Malachy, who died in 1148, there is an incident where Malachy cures the wife of a local noble in Cloyne at the request of Nehemiah, 'bishop of that city'.[30] This same Nehemiah – again as bishop of Cloyne – features in *Visio Tnugdali*, the most famous of the *Schottenkloster* texts.[31] This presents Tnugdalus as a soldier in the service of Cormac Mac Carthaig, king of Munster, who experiences a vision of paradise where he meets king Cormac and several of the now deceased leading 'reform' clerics of the period, including Nehemiah, who is said to have died in his see at an advanced age. This document was written in 1149. This reference gives a clue to the real identity of bishop Nehemiah, who must be the Giolla na Naomh Ua Muircheartaig, *uasale-*

---

29 For at least part of the eleventh century both Múscraige's appear to have shared the same regnal family (Uí Donnocáin) and the usage of the term without a qualifier suggests both kingdoms were periodically united, while on the ecclesiastical side note the associations between the Múscraige saint Laichtín and Donoughmore, Grenagh and Kilnamartra in the southern Múscraige and with Ballyhay in the northern one. (*AI* 1010.7, 1029.3, 1045.11, 1096.6; RIA Ms 23 P I, 948; *CSH* 665.3.7; Maziere-Brady i, lxvii–lxix.) **30** Lawlor, 89 and n. **31** Wagner, 53.

scop deisceirt Ereann, seanoir ogh eccnaidhe cráibhdheach 'noble bishop of
the south of Ireland, a chaste, wise and pius senior', whose death is
recorded in the Annals of the Four Masters, *sub anno* 1149. A further reference to Nehemiah/ Giolla na Naomh occurs in the necrology of the
Schottenkloster of Würzburg, Germany, where he is described *as Nehemias
episcopus et monachus Hyberniae* and, in a related calendar, *Nemias episcopus et monachus nostre congregationis*.[32] From these entries it would seem
that Giolla na Naom, originally an Irish monk of the *Schottenkloster* of
Würzburg, founded in 1134, had served as bishop of Cloyne from sometime during the 1140s or earlier until his death in 1148/9. What are we
to make of this evidence?

The tendency to regard the synods of Ráith Breasail (1111) and Kells-
Mellifont (1152) as marking the exclusive reordering of Irish diocesan
boundaries in this period seems to be unwise. The case of the elevation
of Clonmacnoise to diocesan status outside of the synod of Ráith Breasail
may not have been an isolated one. In a Munster context the monolithic
kingdom of Muirchertach Ua Briain of 1111 had, by 1152, been replaced
by a province divided into two equal and competing polities, Tuadmuma
and Desmuma, under their Uí Briain and Meic Carthaig rulers respectively. This political fragmentation was reflected at Kells-Mellifont in a
corresponding ecclesiastical fragmentation where the seven dioceses of
1111 were replaced by the twelve recognized in 1152.[33] In the case of
Cloyne, and perhaps in some other dioceses, this fragmentation and
reorganization of the boundaries of 1111 certainly pre-dated 1152, at which
synod it was merely acknowledged. In light of the references adduced
above to bishop Giolla na Naomh it would seem likely that the true
father of the 'reformed' diocese of Cloyne was none other than king
Cormac Mac Carthaig (1123–38).

Cormac had succeeded his brother, Tadg, as king of Desmuma in
1123. Four years later he became the first Eóganacht king of Munster
after one and a half centuries, a position he held until his assassination
in 1138. Cormac's support for ecclesiastical reform is well documented.

---

32 Ó Riain-Raedel 1984, 392–3. **33** *PRIA* 26 C, p. 18.

Friend of St Malachy, the Irish reform leader, for whom he founded a monastery in Desmuma; builder of 'Cormac's Chapel' at Cashel, that jewel of Hiberno-Romanesque architecture showing German influences; and major financial supporter of the Irish monasteries in Germany and Austria known as *Schottenkloster*; it is highly unlikely that any significant diocesan reorganization could have occurred in Munster without his approval.[34] The likely connexions between Cormac and Giolla na Naomh are easily discernable. *Visio Tnugdali* is, among other things, a piece of pro-Meic Carthaig propaganda, written at Regensburg during the abbacy of a Mac Carthaig abbot, and designed to enhance the memory of Cormac as a great church reformer. Its inclusion of such noted reformers as Malachy, Cellach of Armagh and Christianus of Louth, in addition to Giolla na Naomh of Cloyne, suggests both an association between Cormac and Giolla na Naomh and that the latter was a churchman and reformer of considerable distinction, as further indicated by his obituary. Indeed the latter has led Gwynn to suggest that Giolla na Naomh 'may have overshadowed the contemporary bishop of Cork'.[35] The Uí Muirchertaig were a regnal family of Eóganacht Locha Léin but of more significance here must be Giolla na Naomh's earlier monastic career in Germany, given the demonstrably close links between Cormac and the Irish *Schottenkongregation* in Germany.[36] It would seem then that, sometime between 1134 and 1138, Cormac Mac Carthaig may have been instrumental in the appointment of Giolla na Naomh as bishop of Cloyne. While this gives us a probable and approximate *terminus ad quem* for the refoundation of the diocese of Cloyne it does not help fix the *terminus a quo*, which could have been at any time since the collapse of Uí Briain power in 1118, for Giolla na Naomh may not have been its first bishop. One suspects this to have been the case, however.

What of the political correlations here? The Uí Briain polity in Munster which had established the new diocesan structures in 1111 collapsed seven years later. The dioceses of Cork, Lismore and Emly all

34 Lawlor, 21–2, 40, 43; Jefferies, 84–8; Ó Riain-Raedel 1984, 401–2. **35** Gwynn, 236. **36** Ó Riain-Raedel 1984, 401–2.

came to lie within the new Meic Carthaig kingdom of Desmuma. As all
three had benefitted from the earlier dismemberment of the *paruchia* of
Cloyne one cannot imagine them being content, let alone proactive in
the re-establishment of Cloyne and we should look for a political motive
for an explanation here. I have already alluded to the major significance
within Desmuma of the Uí Chaím at this time, sponsors of the cult of
Colmán mac Léinín and of his church of Cloyne (6.3). I suspect the re-
establishment of the diocese of Cloyne owes much to the desire for such
a development by the Uí Chaím, the benefits to whose local power are
obvious, as well perhaps to that of other local groups, such as the kings
of Uí Meic Caille. We might even go so far as to postulate a time-range
for this development, the period 1134–38, when the earlier divisions
between the Uí Chaím and Cormac MacCarthaig had been healed and
before the latter's death.[37] This, of course, is the same period as that in
which bishop Giolla na Naomh may have been consecrated for Cloyne.
One final observation may be relevance here. Jefferies has suggested that
the Meic Carthaig had converted the petty-kingdom of Múscraige Mitíne
to mensal land during the 1120s.[38] While the evidence adduced in support of this is not conclusive it certainly warrants serious consideration.
If this were, indeed, the case then a desire for an ecclesiastical re-union
with their cousins north of the Blackwater and the re-establishment of
the *status quo* as it had clearly existed for some centuries before 1111 would
further explain why, in the interests of keeping yet another group of his
subjects happy, Cormac MacCarthaig may have established the diocese
of Cloyne with the same borders as that of its old *paruchia*. The above
conclusion, I believe, accords better with the evidence than that arrived
at by Ó Riain, who suggests that the extent of the 'reformed' diocese of
Cloyne reflects a Meic Carthaig policy of the early 1150s to maintain
control of Fir Maige and Uí Liatháin in the face of the peripherality of
both Emly and Lismore.[39]

---

37 *AI* 1127.6, 1128.3; *MIA* 1123.2, 1128.2, 1135.2. **38** Jefferies, 91–2. **39** Ó Riain 1997a, 94. The
political history of Desmuma in the generations before the Anglo-Norman invasion has not
yet received satisfactory attention from scholars. My forthcoming 'The Rise of the Meic
Carthaig and the Political Geography of Desmumu', in *Peritia* 16, will attempt partly to redress
this situation.

What of the response of those churches which suffered loss as a result of the re-establishment of the diocese of Cloyne? It would seem that both Lismore and Emly – both firmly within the Meic Carthaig orbit at this period – may have been compensated by the reward of a continuing role for their personnel in the ecclesiastical governance of Cloyne. As we have seen already, Emly was the major church most closely associated with Cloyne, and seems to have exercised some kind of metropolitan authority over Cloyne in the pre-'reform' period. Bishop Ua Muircheartaig may have been succeeded at Cloyne by an Emly candidate in the person of Ua Dubchróin, 'bishop and abbot of Cloyne', whose death is recorded in 1159. Another senior cleric with Emly connexions was Diarmait Ua Laígenáin, *fer léginn* or chief teacher/ professor of the school of Cloyne, slain by the Uí Ciarmhaic in 1162. Both surnames are native to the Emly (Eóganacht Áine) area and Ua Laígenáin appears to have been slain in that area, for its kings were the Uí Ciarmhaic. The style 'bishop and abbot' used of Ua Dubchróin is interesting and may simply represent an 'old style' description of the new post-'reform' situation where the bishop had control of temporalities as well as spiritualities, bearing in mind the usage range applicable to the word 'abbot' as illustrated above (9.2). It might finally be noted in relation to Emly that from the middle of the twelfth century onwards, while remaining in the Meic Carthaig kingdom of Desmuma, it lay on the border with and was partly surrounded by Uí Briain territory and must have been very dependent on Meic Carthaig patronage to survive. There is evidence from this period that the Meic Carthaig actually attempted to promote the interests of the hereditary clergy of Emly in the efforts of the latter to control the new diocese of Cashel.[40] Such clear dependence on the support of the Meic Carthaig suggests that the Emly clerical establishment was unlikely to resist Meic Carthaig policy elsewhere. As to the Lismore connexion, Bishop Ua Flandacán of Cloyne, whose death is recorded *sub anno* 1167, bears an important Déisi surname, the modern O'Flanagan.[40a]

---

40 Ó Riain-Raedel 1982, 231. **40a** Curtis, 3; *MIA* 1142.2.

This leaves just Cork to consider, and here the absence of evidence makes arriving at a conclusion difficult. Ó Riain has argued cogently for a date during the last years of the twelfth century for the composition of the Latin Life of Finbarr, which would render it irrelevant in relation to the present question.[41] The crux of the matter is one of interpretation of the evidence given in the Life. Do we see in this a claim to super-territorial diocesan overlordship under the guise of a pattern of alleged foundations by its subject, or should we simply see the list of churches highlighted in both *Vita* and near-contemporary *Beatha* as actual churches belonging to the *paruchia* of Cork, some as separated fragments in the midst of other *paruchiae,* or indeed as a blend of both?[42] Those churches occuring in both sources which lie outside of the diocese of Cork may in fact represent both types of claim. Among the several churches in Ross associated with Finbarr is that of Rosscarbery itself, thus suggesting that the entire diocese of Ross was being claimed here, in marked contrast to Cloyne, where a scattering of individual churches, none with any particular association with Colmán, is claimed (and at least one of which had a linkage with Finbarr, see 8.3). In addition those churches listed in Leinster are, as Ó Riain has shown, merely the claim to jurisdiction over Ross restated in another guise. The apparent claim to all of Ross and the inclusion of at least two churches in Múscraige Mitíne may in fact echo claims to the extent of the diocese of Cork as delimited at Ráith Breasail and thus suggest a date somewhere in the first half of the twelfth century for the *Vita* of Finbarr, as suggested by Ó Corráin.[43] As against this the evidence for linkage beween the *Vita* and the Decretal Letter of 1199, and thus a late date for the former, is substantial.[44] Whatever of all of this, it is clear that Cork's claim to Ross was taken much more seriously by its own propagandists than any to Cloyne. This should perhaps be viewed in light of my earlier suggestion of Cork exercising some kind of metropolitan authority over Ross in the pre-'reform' period. In any case the leadership of the church of Cork appears to have been in dispute between

---

41 Ó Riain 1985, 2–4. **42** Ó Riain 1985, 6; 1994, 62, 67–71, 76, 132, 134; and see 8.3 above. **43** Ó Riain 1997a, 86–7; Ó Corráin 1978, 31. **44** Ó Riain 1985, 3–4, 9; 1994, 35; 1997a, passim.

rival local and Uí Briain candidates during the period immediately after 1138 and so this church may have been in no position to attend to the loss of part of its territory to Cloyne.[45]

One final area pertinent to the boundaries between Cork and Cloyne needs addressing. While in general Irish diocesan boundaries of the twelfth century agree closely with secular political and administrative boundaries this is not entirely the case with that strangely shaped section of Cork north of the Lee which juts up into the belly of Cloyne in such a dramatic fashion. Ó Buachalla thought this might be accounted for by Uí Mathgamna expansion northwards at the expense of Uí Liatháin during the eleventh century and, while this is a clever theory worthy of such a talented historian, it does not accord with the evidence.[46] The sub-infeudation of this area under the Anglo-Normans reveals an interesting picture. While the entire cantred of Olethan (Uí Liatháin) was enfeoffed to the Barry family they, in turn, enfeoffed the Prendergasts with one moiety of Olethan, known to the Normans as Ocurbleithan (from Uí Chuirb Liatháin: this people were, of course, a segment of the larger Uí Liatháin group). This feudal arrangement was echoed in the civil administration of the area, for, although Olethan was usually administered as a single cantred it would appear in fact to have been originally organized into the distinct cantreds of Olethan and Ocurbleithan, corresponding to the manors of Carrigtwohill and Shandon respectively.[47] There is evidence from the pre-invasion period to suggest that Shandon may represent a demesne territory or *tríucha céad* of the Meic Carthaig kings of Desmuma, while the position of Carrigtwohill is uncertain. What is clear is that the Normans, who certainly based their feudal grants on older Irish units of polity, treated both manors as part of an older unity, which argues against Ó Buachalla's interpretation. Ecclesiastically this division into distinct cantreds was echoed exactly in a division between two rural deaneries, also named Olethan and Ocurbleithan, the latter lying in Cloyne, the former in

45 Ó Corráin 1985a; Ó Riain 1997a, 46. **46** Ó Buachalla 1945a, 25–6. **47** Mac Cotter 1996, 76; 2000, 51.

Cork.[48] I suspect the answer to this riddle may lie in a much earlier period, and can be found in *Beatha Bharra*. In this Áed mac Mianach is made a donor of lands north of the Lee to Finbarr. As the author has taken his name out of an early genealogy of Uí Chuirb Liatháin we can be sure that this is a device to explain possession of these lands by the church of Cork in the twelfth century.[49] Given the proximity of these lands to Cork I think it is likely that this device actually commemmorates – whatever of its literal truth – an early donation or association between the Uí Chuirb Liatháin and the church of Cork, probably going back several centuries to a period when the growth of ecclesiastical *paruchiae* was in its early stages and Cork and Cloyne were not the competing mother-churches they would later become. As against this, twelfth-century Meic Carthaig interference in the shape of the 'reformed' dioceses in including their demesne territories in Cork rather than Cloyne cannot be entirely ruled out.

48 Sweetman, 276, 308; Nicholls, 112, which shows that the Meic Carthaig gallows was located at the castle of Sean Dún in the pre-invasion period, suggesting that here lay their capital at Cork. **49** Ó Riain 1994, 73, 142, 259 note 246.

CHAPTER TEN

The legacy of Colmán Mac Léinín

Colmán mac Léinín was certainly a remarkable man. Monk and *fili*, he forged an association with one of Munster's most powerful early kings resulting in his establishment of several important churches where spiritual life continued long after his death and where his memory was long venerated. Secondly, he was long remembered as one of the fathers of Irish literature and poetry, a memory continued and reinforced by the very classical Gaelic bardic tradition of which he may be considered one of the founders. In a more worldly way his cult was hitched to the fortunes of one of Munster's leading royal lineages, a relationship which continued long after the reduction of that lineage to the status of mere local kings. Finally this relationship seems to have led in turn to the patronage of one of Munster's greatest kings and leaders, Cormac Mac Carthaig, whose actions probably ensured the continuence of Colmán's cult in the form of the diocese of Cloyne.

Thus far the account above. What of the later history of this legacy? The arrival of the culturally arrogant Anglo-Normans rudely shattered the ancient cultural homogeneity of the Irish and their church. In Cloyne the chief church was replaced by a large, undistinguished cathedral which, happily, is still in excellent repair. Initially the policy of 'out with the old, in with the new' did not extend to the old Irish ecclesiastical families, whose members continued to hold high position – bishops, deans, etc., – into the early fourteenth century. Ominously, however, those hereditary clerical families and *manaig*-descended betagh families occupying outlying church estates were already beginning to be pushed aside in favour of cadet lines of powerful families of colonial extraction in the east of the diocese by the late thirteenth century, and would soon descend into obscurity and even extinction. Of course no such colonization would be experienced in the western parts of the diocese untouched by colonial settlement, and here, such ancient erenagh families as, among others, the Uí Éalaithaig at Donoughmore and the Uí Ionmhainéin at Tullylease would continue to flourish and thrive until finally dispossessed by the regime of Cromwell centuries later.[1]

The large amount of property owned by the diocese in the Anglo-Norman period, much of which must have been the earlier property of the mother-church of Cloyne, was already under threat from rapacious magnates in the fourteenth century, a pressure which must, at least in part, have resulted in the composition of the well-known *Pipe Roll of Cloyne* (1364). The collapse of what remained of government power in Munster in the early fifteenth century reduced the province to government by the strongest magnates, which in turn led to increased pressure on the cross-lands, a situation not helped by the union of the dioceses of Cork and Cloyne in 1429. Political chaos was followed by ecclesiastical chaos and, at one time in the fifteenth century, the bishopric of the united dioceses of Cork and Cloyne was in contention between no less than three candidates. The eventual winner of this dispute was a Geraldine from the hinterland of Cloyne itself (Garrett FitzGerald), who would rule his sees from the ancient episcopal palace in Cloyne.[2] His success, however, merely delayed the inevitable and, indeed, was a contributory factor to it, in that it led to the consecration of another Geraldine as his successor (his grand-nephew), who, in turn, installed a Geraldine cousin as dean of Cloyne in the early sixteenth century. This dean, while probably in minor orders, was not a celibate and was the founder of a powerful Geraldine ecclesiastical lineage based in Cloyne itself, and whose wealth was based on the usurped cross-lands of the ecclesiastical manor of Cloyne. Thus once again did a lineage rise to power on the back of the wealth of the church of Cloyne. For over a century these hereditary deans of Cloyne ruled their petty-kingdom from the town, their power increasing to its apogee in the time of the last dean, John fitz Edmund. Not alone did he succeed in legalizing his *de facto* inherited possession of the Cloyne estate, but he also succeeded in

---

1 *PRC* xii–xiii, 202–5, 219–20, 224–5. 2 For this and what follows in the paragraph see Mac Cotter, forthcoming.

obtaining the bulk of what remained of the ancient cross-lands throughout the diocese, which were then sold off to local magnates. Fitz Edmund made himself an indispensable ally of the New English administration, then engaged in virtually a reconquest and recolonization of Munster, and, as a *quid pro quo*, a blind eye was turned to his alienation and usurpation of the lands of the church. Such was his local power that, remarkably, the arrival of the Established Church in Cloyne was delayed by thirty years and it only obtained possession of the cathedral and its precincts in 1613 upon the old dean's death. Surprisingly, Fitz Edmund, in spite of his loyalty to Elizabeth I, was a Catholic, and used much of his wealth to support that church unobtrusively. It is surely fitting that such a significant leader in Cloyne's history is commemorated by a fine tomb which may still be seen in Cloyne cathedral.

Once eventually established in Cloyne the Anglican Church soon separated the united dioceses and Cloyne was once again independent (in 1638). Its efforts to recover its lost lands were greatly hampered by the wars of 1641–52 and, eventually, only a small portion of the ancient possessions of the see were recovered.[3] The bishop's palace in Cloyne, earlier the seat of the Geraldine bishops and deans, was graced by several noble and humane incumbents whose contribution to knowledge and letters is well known and whose associations still bring lustre to Cloyne. Only one bishop is cast in a dubious light in relation to stewardship of the ancient holy places of Cloyne, and this was Bishop Charles Crowe (1702–26). An enduring local tradition, first recorded by Windele early in the nineteenth century, and still current in the area to this very day, attributes to Crowe the deliberate destruction of what appears to have been an ancient oratory in the grounds of the cathedral, believed by the local populace to house the remains of Colmán mac Léinín himself. Crowe's actions are attributed to distaste at an annual pilgrimage or pattern where the pious prayed at the saint's tomb. The building was said to have been reduced almost to ground level and what had been dug up from the interior carted off to Ballycroneen and thrown into the

---

3 Maziere-Brady, iii, 7-21.

sea. Some support for this tradition comes from recent archaeological investigations into the remains of this oratory or 'fire house', which found only burials post-dating Crowe's episcopate. Such an action would not have been out of place in one of the most sectarian and disturbed periods of Irish history, and Crowe is known to have referred to his Catholic fellow-townsmen as 'Teagues'.[4] Such philistine iconoclasticism, as one would expect, was very much the exception and the record over several centuries rather shows clearly the continued and expensive commitment to maintaining the fabric of cathedral and precinct by Cloyne's Church of Ireland community. The last Anglican bishop of Cloyne died in 1835, after which the diocese was united with those of Cork and Ross, the care of the sacred precincts devolving upon the deanery of Cloyne.

The Roman Catholic church experienced centuries of disturbance and travail following its expulsion from Cloyne cathedral, an event still remembered in local tradition as recorded during the 1930s, when the priests were said to have been driven from the cathedral by soldiers during mass and were later forced to say mass in the local caves.[5] Once somewhat more enlightened times arrived, the renewed structures of the church saw Cork and Cloyne again separated (in 1747) and the seat of Cloyne established in Cove (Cóbh) during the episcopacy of Matthew McKenna (1769–91), who had earlier been parish priest there.[6] Here during the later part of the nineteenth century a magnificent cathedral, dedicated to Colmán, would be built.

One final legacy of Colmán mac Léinín is his remembrance in folk memory. Perhaps surprisingly, this is confined to the area around Cloyne itself, where a number of tales survive in relation to the saint. One of these tales concerns the saint building the round-tower. While building it in the course of one night the saint, now almost finished and the dawn

---

4 Maziere-Brady, iii, 115; Zajac, et al, 33; Coleman, 142; Schools Folklore Collection, UCD, 382/140. **5** Schools Folklore Collection, UCD, 382/140. These memories may preserve some actual memory of the recovery of the Cathedral by the Catholics during the period 1642–9. **6** During the Penal Era there was no established seat and such diocesan administration as was possible was carried out from the home of whatever parish the resident bishop resided in. The choice of Cove seems to derive from McKenna's position as parish priest here before his elevation.

rising, was hailed by a woman inquiring as to what he was doing. As her inquiry was made in an ill-mannered way the saint got into a rage and, leaping from the round-tower, landed one and a half miles away at Lurrig on a stone, leaving the imprints of his knees on the stone. Another version of this story has the saint leaping, in fright from the woman's interruption, to Kilva and then to Glen Iris wood (in Bawnard East townland, two miles north-west of Cloyne), where, in thirst, he prayed to God to provide water whereupon a spring gushed forth where one had never been before, the origin of St Colman's holy well. A pattern was still held here during the octave of the saint's feast in the 1930s, attended 'by only a few nowadays'. The well is said to provide a cure for rheumatism. Again the saint is associated with his sister, Macha, the traditional eponym of Kilva, whose name is pronounded locally as 'Vaw'. Both were said to live together in a house here, where the imprint of the saint's knees, due to his praying, could still be seen on a stone. This story centers around the remains of an ancient church here.[7] I have been unable to locate traditions concerning the saint elsewhere in the diocese.

This study has, I hope, presented a clear picture of this early and interesting saint. For historians his *persona* provides some insight, however imperfect, into life at the very beginning of recorded Irish history, and the history of his cult reveals much about both secular and ecclesiastical politics in Munster during the 'Dark Ages'. For the devout, Colmán's heritage is shared between both Christian traditions in the diocese and his work provided the foundation for centuries of Christian life in Cloyne. Such an important early Christian leader is surely deserving of remembrance or veneration as one chooses.

7 Schools Folklore Collection, UCD, 382/138; 394/222–3.

Bishops of South Munster before AD 1100

Church	Annals from	Quality	7th	8th	9th	10th	11th
Ardfert	1032	Broken	–	–	–	–	1
Cloyne	697	Broken	–	–	2	–	–
Cork	682	Near continuous	–	–	2	2	4
Emly	630	Near continuous	1	–	1	2	1
Lismore	637	Near continuous	1	1	–	2	–
Rosscarbery	824	Broken	–	–	–	–	1
Scattery	792	Broken	–	1	–	2	–

The dates given are those when annalistic coverage begins, after which its quality is described. The remaining columns indicate the number of bishops recorded in association with the relevant church in each century between the seventh to the eleventh. The columns from the seventh to the tenth centuries are based on Etchingham's *Church organization in Ireland: AD 650 to 1000*, Maps 2 to 5. The seventh-century episcopal reference from Emly is indirect in that it derives from mention of 'the successor of bishop Ailbe' in a document which can be securely dated to 630.[1] The only important church centre in the area – to judge by quality of annalistic record – not associated with a bishop was Mungret. *AI* 1079.2 records the obituary of one bishop Ua Suarlig who 'rested in Ardpatrick'. As he is not described as 'bishop of Ardpatrick' in this ambiguous entry I have not included him in the table above.

1 Walsh 1988, 90.

Distribution of the cults of Colmán and associates, and Finbarr of Cork

The results of this distribution study are represented in Map 2. The evidence pertaining to the cult of Finbarr is given as a comparison to that given for Colmán and associated cults. Evidence for cult associations can be found in the dedications of individual churches and holy wells to particular saints, often preserved in the very name of the church or well. In the case of ecclesiastical dedications I believe that all those to native saints must pre-date the Anglo-Norman invasion, as there is clear evidence that the latter introduced their own dedicatory patterns, either to national saints such as David or to the apostles or the Blessed Virgin Mary. There were many Colmáns, or course, and only those dedications which can be confirmed by some temporal association with the diocese of Cloyne can be taken as reasonably certain.

The cult of Colmán

Churches and wells certainly dedicated to the saint are as follows:

- Cloyne, a parish and episcopal seat.

- Ballynacorra parish, barony of Imokilly. A charter of the 1190s names this church as *ecclesiam sancti Colmani de Cor*.[2] The dedication does not appear subsequently.

- Kilmaclenine parish, barony of Orrery & Kilmore.

- Farrahy parish, barony of Fermoy. This dedication is attested by early eighteenth century inscription on the Anglican church ruin here and later in that century by Bishop McKenna for the Roman Catholic tradition. Its antiquity is demonstrated in that Farrahy (Bearn Mic Íomhair) was a prebend of the treasurer of Cloyne in the thirteenth century.[3]

2 Gilbert, 200. 3 Grove-White, 115; Maziere-Brady i, lxvii–lxix; Sweetman, 311.

- St Colman's Well, Bawnard East, Ballynacorra parish, Imokilly barony. Rounds or a pattern was held at this well during the octave of Colmán Mac Léinín until at least the 1930s.[4]

- St Colman's Well, Ballinbrittig, Carrigtwohill parish, Barrymore barony.

- Colmanswell parish and holy well, Connello Upper Barony, Co. Limerick. This was the ancient parish of Cluain Comharda or Cloncourth, already divided between the dioceses of Limerick and Cloyne in the earliest Anglo-Norman records. From the Pipe Roll of Cloyne it is clear that this ecclesiastical division was echoed in the temporalities of the dioceses, the same tenant holding the entire fee of both sees. As late as 1503 the parish was still divided into two vicarages, one each in Limerick and in Cloyne. In modern times the dedication to Colmán of Cloyne was forgotten and instead Colmán mac Duach was commemorated here.[5]

- Kilcolman, Kilshannig parish, Duhallow barony. This was among the cross-lands of Cloyne.

- Kilcolman, the obsolete name for Knockardamrum, parish of Ballyhay, barony of Orrery & Kilmore.[6] This was among the cross-lands of Cloyne.

Possible dedications to the saint are as follows:

- Kilcolman, Doneraile parish, Fermoy barony. This church is recorded as *Cill Colmain Grec* in the pre-Norman *Crichad an Chaoilli*.[7] In company with Canon Power I can find no reference to any Colmán Grec; can the qualifier be to distinguish this Cill Colmáin from those at Knockardamrum a few miles to the west and Farrahy to the east?

---

4 Schools Folklore Collection, UCD, 394/222–3. **5** *PRC*, 112–121, 202; Fuller, 576; Begley, 97. **6** Book of Survey and Distribution. **7** Power 1932, 49.

- Kilcolman, Magourney parish, Muskerry East barony. The nineteenth century civil parish of Magourney is an amalgam of two older parishes, that of Magourney proper and that of Sean Chaisleáin (Old Castle), whose shape is preserved in that of the northern salient of Magourney, and whose church was located in Kilcolman townland. In 1492 the vicarage of Sean Chaisleáin was dedicated to 'Saint Colinary', apparently Colmán *plus* qualifier. This rendering is, however, too corrupt to make much of and, given the normally poor scribal standard of the source, it may simply refer to a Colmán. The eighteenth-century Catholic parish of Magourney (Coachford) was dedicated to Colmán of Cloyne. Cf. Ó Riain's suggested possible association between Colmán of Daire Dúnchon (unidentified) in *Beatha Bharra* and this Kilcolman.[8]

- Kilcolman, Dromtariff parish, Duhallow barony. While in the present – and medieval – diocese of Kerry this denomination lies just across the river from the cross-lands of Clonmeen in Cloyne and there is evidence of boundary instability in this area in the pre-Norman period between the Áes Aella and Múscraige.[9]

- Tobar Colmáin well, Kilfrush townland and parish, Small County barony, Co. Limerick. Recorded on the first Ordnance Survey map as 'St Brigit's Well', in spite of an earlier attestation to Colmán, this holy well lies just three miles west of Emly and in the very heart of the area which I have shown above to have been Colmán's native territory. The only Saint Colmán who can be shown to have any associations with the area is Mac Léinín and this well may represent an ancient memory of his cult in his homeland. The double association here is most interesting in light of my comments below regarding a possible cult of Brigit, sister of Colmán, in Cloyne. There was also a well dedicated to Brigit in Kilteely near Kilfrush.[10]

- There are several other Kilcolman's in the surrounding counties of Limerick, Tipperary, Waterford and Kerry but no particular associ-

---

8 Haren, 449; Maziere-Brady i, lxvii–lxix; Ó Riain 1994, 247 note 166.   **9** See my 'Cantred and Tríucha Céad', forthcoming.   **10** Ó Danachair, 216.

ation between these and our saint can be established. The Kilcolmans in the parishes of Ringrone and Desertserges in the diocese of Cork probably represent dedications to Colmán Ailithir of Ross rather than to Mac Léinín.

Cults associated with Colmán

Colmán's sister, Macha or Machain, is commemorated in Kilmahon Parish, Imokilly Barony, as recorded by McKenna, and in the townland of Kilva in Cloyne Parish, both toponyms on record in the thirteenth century.[11] In the case of the latter the association is remembered in local folklore.

Another of the saint's sisters was Brigit. Unfortunately the ubiquitousness of the cult of the much more famous Brigit of Kildare clouds the picture in relation to dedications to this saint in Co. Cork. As almost all such dedications occurring in Cloyne are associated with what was once cross-land we should perhaps be slow to dismiss these as representing a commemoration to Brigit, sister of Mac Léinín. Can this pattern be pure coincidence? There are also a number of churches and wells dedicated to a Brigit in the dioceses of Cork and Ross. Cloyne parish churches dedicated to Brigit as recorded by McKenna in the eighteenth century are Britway (Barrymore Barony) and Buttevant (Orrery & Kilmore Barony), both part of the ancient church-lands of Cloyne. The dedication at Buttevant is first recorded in 1366. Both parishes have corresponding holy well dedications (in Britway and Mount Brigit), although the latter well had a pattern associating it with Brigit of Kildare. The one exception to this pattern is the holy well dedicated to a Brigit in Clonfert (townland and parish), barony of Duhallow, which was not cross-land.[12]

The cult of Finbarr of Cork

In Map 2 I have also illustrated the distribution of this cult as I believe it to represent the ancient *paruchia* of Cork just as does that of Colmán

---

11 Brooks, 329; Sweetman, 275.   **12** Maziere-Brady, i, lxvii–lxix; *PRC* 54; Power 1994, 173; 2000, 459–50, 467.

Cloyne, and the comparison is illuminating. Here we have, of course, Cork, and then several Kilbarrys. These occur in the parishes of St Ann's Shandon, Fanlobbus, Templemartin, Kilmoe, Inchigeelagh and Ballinadee. The onomastic and feudal history of these townlands, apart from the last, suggests that these probably represent genuine dedications to Finbarr. In addition one should certainly add Gúgán Barra, Farranavarrigane in Macloneigh parish, the eponym of which was Finbarr's father, Amairgen, and Kilnaglery which housed relics of Finbarr in 1088.[13] There are two Kilbarrys which appear not to derive from the form *Ceall Bharra* and which should therefore not be included on a cult map for Finbarr. This is especially important as both lie within the diocese of Cloyne. As Ó Riain has identified one as deriving from Ceall Bharra and muted the possibility in the case of the other, comment is necessary.[14]

Kilbarry, Castlelyons Parish. Ó Riain rejects Power's derivation from the Barry family[15] in favour of that of Ceall Bharra, which he suggests is to be identified with the church of 'Cenn Droma of Carn Tigernaig' in *Beatha Bharra*. This identification is untenable. Power was on the right track with his suggestion that the adjacent and nearly equal denominations of Kilbarry and Kilmagner represent an older *baile* divided between these Anglo-Norman families. While this entire section of Castlelyons Parish had passed to various Condon families by the late sixteenth century originally it must have formed part of the de Barry demesne manor of Castellolethan and was in the contemporary cantred of Olethan. The first element in both denominations must represent *Coill*, as evidenced by the form Keillynemagnearie from 1611, and both seem to have been divisions of one original super-denomination, described in 1630 as 'the territory and cantred of Kilbarry alias Aghegranagh' when income from its 'tymbers and woods' was singled out for mention. Earlier, in 1595, there is mention of 'the woods of Kilbarry'. It would appear that the present townland of Kilbarry represents the purchases of the earl of Cork from the Condons here, who retained Ballydorgan. The church site in

---

13 *AI* 1088.2. **14** Ó Riain 1977, 78; 1994, 254; 1997a, 34. **15** Power 1932, 70. Ó Buachalla (1949, 32) also gives this derivation.

the modern Kilbarry is actually in the sub-denomination of Ballyclough, listed in 1611 as a distinct townland.[16]

Kilbarry, Kilbrin Parish. This has the same derivation, *Coill a' Bharraig*, as does Kilbarry in Castlelyons. All of Kilbrin was originally a Barry fee and the form Kilvarrig from 1656 is indisputable.[17]

16 Ó Buachalla 1967, 63, note 37; *Calendar of the Irish patent rolls* (Dublin, 1966), 194; Brewer and Bullen, 487; Grosart, 62–3. 17 Book of Survey and Distribution.

The poems of Colmán
A new translation by Professor Donnchadh Ó Corráin

COLMÁN MAC LÉINÍN
Fragments edited by R. Thurneysen, 'Colmán mac Léníne und Senchán Torpéist', *Z Celt Philol* 19 (1933) 193–209.

4 Luin oc elaib	'Blackbirds compared with swans
4 ungi oc dīrnaib	ounces compared with pounds
5 drecha ban n-athech	the faces of peasants' wives
5 oc rōdaib rīgnaib	compared with glorious queens
4 rīg oc Domnall	kings compared with Domnall
4 dord oc aidbse	humming compared with choral singing
5 adand oc caindill	a rushlight compared with a candle
5 calg oc mo chailgse	any sword compared with my sword.'

II.

3 Dūn maic Daim	'The fortress of Mac Daim
3 doë ōs roi	a fortress over the plain
2 ronn tart	a dribble of thirsts
2 tacht coí	a choking of lamentations.'

Could this be Áed Damán (633)?

IIIA

4 Ó ba mac cléib	'Since he was a child in the cradle
3 caindlech ser	the bright star
3 sirt cach n-ainm	the name of Man-Strength
4 ainm gossa fer	surpassed every name.'

The reference is to Fergus Tuile son of Feradach Dornmár of Uí Liatháin. The son of Fergus, Diucaill, died in 632 – and this would make Fergus an exact contemporary of Colmán, and very possibly king of Uí Liatháin in his time.

IIIB

Indlith d̲ūn	'Harnessed for us
d̲rūb iar m̲ār	after long delay
m̲ag feda d̲ian	the swift wooden plain [chariot]
d̲ian cullian c̲lār	whose plank is holly;
c̲āch dia e̲ol	each to his home
i̲mgland r̲ois	pure of knowledge;
r̲opo d̲oim	Fergus has become for us
d̲ūn Fergus fois.	a house of peace.'

Díucaill, son of Fergus, died in 632; therefore Fergus was an exact contemporary of the poet.

IV

Nī sēim a̲nim	'Not slender the loss
i̲ n-anmib āne	among the losses of fame
ār for Aed Slāne	the slaughter of Aed Sláne.'

This must be an extract from an elegy for Áed Sláne, overking of Uí Néill (604)

V.

Nī for d̲iuchtror for d̲uain *i̲ndlis*
iar cotlud c̲haīn *b̲indris*
b̲riathar chorgais: cen nach n d̲īchmaircc
d̲eog *écndairce, r̲ath *r̲īgmaicc*.

*for Thurneysen's *nepnairc*

'I do not awaken to an improper poem
after a beautiful sweet-dreamed sleep;
a Lenten command: to do nothing unpermitted,
a drink [wine of the Mass] of requiems, the grace of the Royal Son.'

In these examples running words are rendered in italic.

The poet awakes to the holy chant of the church
after sleeping: it is Lent, and the things of Lent are to be done,
obedience, no drink but chalice of requiem masses, and the
earning of the grace of Christ.

VI

Ropo t̲h̲ānaise
t̲riuin c̲r*apscuil*
c̲eirdd p̲romthaidi
P̲etair **axail.*

*For MS apstail

'It was the second twilight watch
[i.e. the second twilight third i.e. the dawn watch]
the manner of testing
of the apostle Peter.'

crapscul <L. crepusculum

This refers to Peter's denial of Christ before cockcrow (Mt 26.34, 26.75;
Mk 14.30, 14.72; Lk 22.34, 22.61).

[VII]

Calvert Watkins has succeeded in reconstructing the fragment cited p.
197.A.1–2: Watkins, Calvert, 'Varia II', *Ériu* 19 (1962) 2. Old Irish *-antar*
(116–18)

Here Watkins edits and translates an extract from: E.J. Gwynn, 'An Old-Irish treatise on the privileges and responsibilities of poets', *Ériu* 13 (1942) 1–60, 220–36: 13.5–6. It occurs in three sources: Gwynn loc. cit.; RIA 23 P 3, 21 (given by Gwynn, ibid.); and BB immediately before poems attrib. to Colmán mac Lénine (Thurneysen, *ZCP* 19 (1933) 197).

> do-aisic a dath
> dia aír -antar
> aiged cach airgit
> acht co ngúairiu -glantar

'It recovers its colour/ if it is blemished by satire/ the face of every silver/ provided it is polished with a bristle'

-antar is 3 sg. pres. of *anaid 'blemishes', a homonym of anaid 'waits, remains' [W. demonstrates this from IE comparisons]. Metre: 5/1, 4/2, 5/2, 6/2; rhyme between b and c, binding alliteration between abcd

Maps

Map 1: Cluain Uama

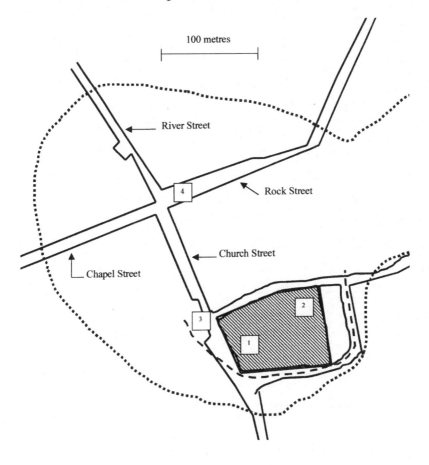

100 metres

River Street

Rock Street

Church Street

Chapel Street

4

3

1

2

1. Cathedral
2. Possible early oratory site ('Fire House')
3. Round Tower
4. Site of medieval market cross

....   Indicates edge of limestone plateau

- - - - -   Indicates probable partial line of inner enclosure

                Hatched area indicates present cathedral precinct

Map 2: Cult sites (Appendix B)

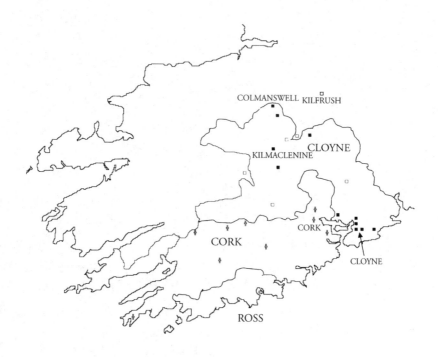

COLMANSWELL KILFRUSH

KILMACLENINE CLOYNE

CORK

CORK

CLOYNE

ROSS

■   Colman and associates, certain
□   Colman and asociates, possible
⚕   Finbarr and associates, both

Maps

Map 3

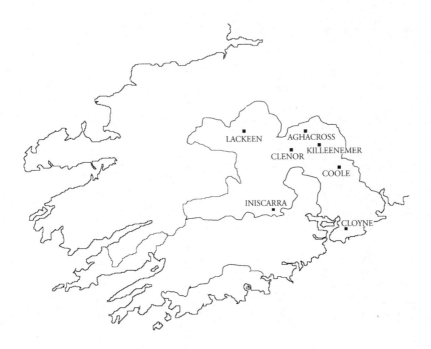

Locations with shared Betagh populations on church lands in
thirteenth–fourteenth century Cloyne

(Possible indicators of earlier extent of Manaig families of *paruchia* of Cloyne: see 8.4)

Map 4

KILLEENEMER
KILMACKENINE
COOLE
DONOUGHMORE
CLOYNE

Primary manors of the Anglo-Norman diocese of Cloyne

Bibliography

Begley, J. (1906): *The diocese of Limerick ancient and modern*. Dublin.

Bergin, O. (1918): 'Unpublished Irish poems, No. 1' in *Studies* 7, 97–99.

____ (1970): *Irish bardic poetry*. Oxford.

Best, R.I., and Lawlor, H.J. (1931): *The Martyrology of Tallaght* (Henry Bradshaw Society 68). London.

____ and O'Brien, M.A. (1954–7): *The Book of Leinster*, 5 volumes. Dublin.

Bhreathnach, E. (1996): 'Temoria: Caput Scotorum?' in *Ériu* 47, 67–88.

Bieler, L. (1979): *Patrician texts in the Book of Armagh*. Dublin.

Brewer, J.S., and Bullen, W. (1869): *Calendar of the Carew manuscripts, 1589–1600*. London.

Brooks, Eric St John (1936): 'Unpublished charters relating to Ireland, 1177–82, from the archives of the city of Exeter', *PRIA* 43 C, 313–66.

Bugge, A. (1905): *Caithreim Cellachain Caisil: The victorious career of Cellachan of Cashel*. Christiana.

Byrne, F.J. (1973): *Irish kings and high-kings*. London. Latest edition Dublin 2000.

____ (1984): 'Heads of churches to c.1200', in Moody et al., *A new history of Ireland*, ix, 237–63. Oxford.

____ (1994); '*Dercu*: the feminine of *Mocu*' in *Éigse* 28, 42–70.

Caerwyn-Williams, J. (1971): *The court poet in medieval Ireland*. Oxford.

Carney, J. (1971): 'Three Old Irish accentual poems' in *Ériu* 22, 23–80.

Charles-Edwards, T.M. (1992): 'The pastoral role of the church in the early Irish laws' in Blair, J., and Sharpe, R., *Pastoral care before the parish*, 63–80. Leicester.

Coleman, J. (1910): 'St Colman of Cloyne', in *JCHAS* 16, 132–142.

Curtis, E. (1929): 'Sheriff's account of the honour of Dungarvan' in *PRIA* 39 C, 1–17.

Dobbs, M. (1930–2): 'The Ban-Seanchus' in *Revue Celtique* 47, 283–339; 48, 163–234; 49, 437–489.

____ (1939): 'Miscellany from H. 2. 7.' in *ZCP* 21, 307–18

Doble, G.H. (1997): *The saints of Cornwall*, i. Facsimile reprint, Felinfach.

Doherty, C. (1980): 'Exchange and trade in early medieval Ireland' in *JRSAI* 110, 67–90.

____ (1985): 'The monastic town in early medieval Ireland' in Clarke, H.B., and Simms, A. (eds), *The comparative history of urban origins in non-Roman Europe*, ii, 45–76. Oxford.

Empey, C.A. (1970): 'The cantreds of medieval Tipperary' in *North Munster Antiquarian Journal* 13, 23–9.

_____ (1981): 'The settlement of the kingdom of Limerick' in Lydon, J. (ed.), *England and Ireland in the later Middle Ages*. Dublin.

_____ (1992): 'Anglo-Norman Waterford' in Nolan, W., and Power, T. (eds), *Waterford history and society*, 131–46. Dublin.

Etchingham, C., (1993): 'The implications of *Paruchia*' in *Ériu* 44, 139–62.

_____ (1994): 'Bishops in the early Irish church: a reassessment' in *Studia Hibernica* 28, 35–62.

_____ (1999): *Church organization in Ireland: AD 650 to 1000*. Maynooth.

Flanagan, D. (1984): 'The Christian impact on early Ireland: placenames evidence' in Ní Catháin, P., and Richter, M. (eds), *Irland und Europa: die Kirche im Frühmittelalter*. Stuttgart.

Fraser, J., Grosjean, P., O'Keefe., J.G. (1931–4): *Irish Texts*, 5 fasc. London.

Fuller, A. (1994): *Calendar of entries in the papal registers relating to Great Britain and Ireland*, xvii/i. Dublin.

Gilbert, J.T. (1889): *Register of the abbey of St Thomas, Dublin*. (Rolls Series). London.

Green, M.J. (1995): 'The gods and the supernatural' in Green, M.J. (ed.), *The Celtic world*, 465–88. London.

Grosart, A. (1886): *The Lismore papers* (1st Series), iii. London.

Grove-White, J. (1913): *Historical and topographical notes, etc.*, iii. Cork.

Gwynn, A. (1992): (ed.) O'Brien, G., *The Irish church in the eleventh and twelfth centuries*. Dublin.

Hardy, T. (1838): *Rotuli chartarum in Turri Londinensi*. London.

Haren, M. (1978): *Calendar of entries in the papal registers relating to Great Britain and Ireland*, xv. Dublin.

Heist, W.W. (1965): *Vitae Sanctorum Hiberniae* (Subsidia Hagiographica 28). Brussells.

Henry, P. (1978): *Saoithiúlacht na Sean-Ghaeilge*. Baile Atha Cliath.

Herbert, M. (1988a): *Iona, Kells and Derry: The history and hagiography of the monastic* familia *of Columba*. Oxford.

_____ (1988b): and Ó Riain, P. (eds), *Betha Adamnáin: the Irish Life of Adamnáin* (Irish Texts Society 54). London.

Hogan, E. (1910): *Onomasticon Goedelicum locorum et tribuum Hiberniae et Scotiae*. Dublin.

Hughes, K. (1954): 'The cult of St Finnian of Clonard from the eighth to the eleventh centuries' in *Irish Historical Studies* 9, 13–27.

_____ (1972): *Early Christian Ireland: introduction to the sources*. Ithaca.

Hull, V. (1947): 'Conall Corc and the Corco Luigde' in *Publications of the Modern Language Association of America* 62, 897–909.

_____ (1958): 'On Conall Corc and the Corco Luigde' in *ZCP* 27, 64–74.

Jefferies, H. (1983): 'Desmond: the early years and the career of Cormac MacCarthy' in *JCHAS* 88, 81–99.

Kelleher, J.V. (1967): 'The rise of the Dál Cais' in Rynne, E. (ed.), *North Munster Studies*, 230–41. Limerick.

Lanigan, J. (1822): *Ecclesiastical history of Ireland*, 4 vols. Dublin.

Lawlor, H.J. (1920): *St Bernard of Clairvaux's Life of St Malachy of Armagh*. London.

McCone, K.R. (1990): *Pagan past and Christian present in early Irish literature*. Maynooth.

MacCotter P. (1996): 'The sub-infeudation and descent of the FitzStephen/Carew moiety of Desmond, Part 1' in *JCHAS* 101, 64–80.

_____ (2000): 'The cantreds of Desmond' in *JCHAS* 105, 49–68.

_____ (forthcoming): 'The Geraldine clerical lineages of Imokilly and Sir John fitz Edmund of Cloyne' in Edwards, D. (ed.), *Regions & rulers in Ireland, c.1100–c.1650*. Dublin.

MacErlean, J. (1914): 'The synod of Ráith Breasail: boundaries of the dioceses of Ireland' in *Archivium Hibernicum* 3, 1–33.

MacNiocaill, G. (1951): *Notitiae as Leabhar Cheanannais*. Baile Atha Cliath.

MacNeill, J. (1911): 'Early Irish population groups: their nomenclature, classification and chronology' in *PRIA* 29 C, 59–114.

MacShamhráin, A. (1996): *Church and polity in pre-Norman Ireland: the case of Glendalough*. Maynooth.

Mazier-Brady, W. (1863–4): *Clerical and parochial records of Cork, Cloyne and Ross*. 3 volumes. Dublin.

Meyer, K. (1905): *Cáin Adamnáin: an Old Irish treatise on the Law of Adamnáin*, (Anecdotia Oxoniensia Medieval and Modern Series, part xii). Oxford.

_____ (1906): *The triads of Ireland*, (Todd Lecture Series 13). Dublin.

_____ (1907): 'The expulsion of the Déssi' in *Ériu* 3, 135–142.

_____ (1910): 'Conall Corc and the Corco Luigde' in Bergin, Best et al., *Anecdota from Irish Manuscripts* 3. Halle.

Moody, T.W., Martin, F.X., Byrne, F.J. (1984): *A new history of Ireland* ix. Oxford.

Nicholls, Kenneth (1972): 'Inquisitions of 1224 from the Miscellanea of the Exchequer' in *Analecta Hibernica* 27, 113–9.

Ní Dhonnchadha, M. (1982): 'The guarantor list of Cáin Adomnáin, 697' in *Peritia* 1, 178–215.

Ní Mhaonaigh, M. (1996): '*Cogad Gáedel re Gallaib* and the Annals' in *Ériu* 47, 101–26.

Ó Buachalla, L. (1939): 'The Uí Liatháin and their septlands' in *JCHAS* 44, 28–36.

_____ (1945a): 'The Uí Mac Caille in pre-Norman times' in *JCHAS* 50, 24–27.

_____ (1945b): 'The ecclesiastical families of Cloyne' in *JCHAS* 50, 83–88.

_____ (1949): 'Placenames of north-east Cork' in *JCHAS* 54, 31–4.

____ (1951–6): 'Contributions towards the political history of Munster, 450–800 AD' in *JCHAS* 56 (1951), 87–90; 57 (1952), 67–86; 59 (1954), 111–26; 61 (1956), 89–102.

____ (1967): 'An early fourteenth-century placename list for Anglo-Norman Cork' in *Dinnseanchas* 3/2, 39–50.

Ó Cathasaigh, T. (1986): 'Curse and Satire' in *Éigse* 21, 10–15.

Ó Coileáin, S. (1983): 'The saint and the king' in de Brún, P., Ó Coileáin, S., Ó Riain, P. (eds), *Folia Gadelica*, 36–46. Cork.

Ó Corráin, D. (1971): 'Topographical notes II' in *Ériu* 22, 97–9.

____ (1972): *Ireland before the Normans*. Dublin.

____ (1973): 'Dál Cais – church and dynasty' in *Ériu* 24, 52–63.

____ (1974): '*Caithréim Challacháin Chaisil*: History or propaganda' in *Ériu* 25, 1–69.

____ (1978): 'Nationality and kingship in pre-Norman Ireland' in Moody, T.W. (ed.), *Nationality and the pursuit of national independence*, 1–35. Belfast.

____ (1979): 'Onomata' in *Ériu* 30, 165–80.

____ (1980): 'Irish kings and high-kings' (Review article) in *Celtica* 13, 150–168.

____ (1981a): 'The early Irish churches: some aspects of organization', in Ó Corráin (ed.), *Irish antiquity*, 327–41. Cork.

____ (1981b): 'Foreign connections and domestic politics: Killaloe and the Uí Briain in twelfth-century hagiography' in Whitlock, Dumville and McKitterick (ed.), *Ireland in early medieval Europe: studies in memory of Kathleen Hughes* (Cambridge), 213–31.

____ et al. (1984): 'Laws of the Irish' in *Peritia* 3, 382–438.

____ (1985a): 'Ecclesiastical power struggle' in Barry et al., *History of Cork* (Cork Examiner, 16 January 1985, p. 8).

____ (1985b): 'The myth and the reality', in Barry et al., *History of Cork* (Cork Examiner, 23 January, 1985, p. 11).

____ (1985c): 'Irish origin legends and genealogy: recurrent aetiologies' in Nyberg, Tore et al. (eds), *History and heroic tale: a symposium*, 51–96. Odense.

____ (1987): 'Irish vernacular law and the Old Testament' in Ní Catháin and Richter (eds), *Irland und die Christenheit*, Stuttgart.

____ (1994): 'The historical and cultural background to the Book of Kells', O'Mahony, F. (ed.), *Proceedings of a conference at Trinity College Dublin, 6–9 September, 1992*, 1–32. Dublin.

____ (1998): 'Creating the past: the early Irish genealogical tradition' in *Peritia* 12, 177–208.

Ó Danachair, C. (1955): 'The holy wells of Co. Limerick' in *JRSAI* 85, 193–217.

O'Doherty, J. (1944): *De Praesulibus Hiberniae ... authore Joanne Linchaeo*, 2 vols. Dublin.

Ó Donnchadha, T. [1940]: *An Leabhar Muimhneach*. Baile Átha Cliath.

O'Hanlon, J. [n.d.]: *Lives of the Irish saints*, iii. Dublin.

O'Keeffe, J.G. (1931): 'Betha Molaga', in Fraser et al., *Irish texts* 3, 1–8, 11–22.

O'Kelleher, A. and Schoepperle, G. (1918): *Betha Colaim Chille*. Illinois.

Olden, Revd T., (1887): 'Saint Colman of Cloyne', in *Dictionary of national biography*, xi, 386–7. London.

Ó Murchadha, D. (1977): 'The Uí Meic Thíre' in *JCHAS* 82, 98–101.

Ó Raithbheartaigh, T. (1932): *Genealogical tracts*, i. Dublin.

Ó Riain, P. (1975): 'The composition of the Irish section of the Calendar of Saints' in *Dinnseanchas* 6, 77–92.

_____ (1977): 'St Finbarr: a study in a cult', *JCHAS* 82, 63–82.

_____ (1978): *Cath Almaine*. Dublin.

_____ (1983): 'Irish saints' genealogies', in *Nomina* 7, 23–29.

_____ (1985): 'Another Cork charter: the Life of Saint Finbarr' in *JCHAS* 90, 1–13.

_____ (1990): 'The Tallaght Martyrologies redated' in *Cambridge Medieval Celtic Studies*, 20, 21–38.

_____ (1994): *Beatha Bharra: Saint Finbarr of Cork, the complete life* (Irish Texts Society 57). London.

_____ (1997a): *The making of a saint: Finbarr of Cork, 600–1200 AD* (Irish Texts Society subsidiary series 5). London.

_____ (1997b): 'When and why *Cothraige* was first equated with *Patricius*?' in *ZCP* 49–50, 698–711.

_____ (2002): 'Irish saints' cults and ecclesiastical families' in Sharpe and Thatcher (eds), *Local saints and local churches in the early medieval West*, 291–303. Oxford.

Ó Riain-Raedel, D. (1982): 'Aspects of the promotion of Irish saints' cults in medieval Germany' in *ZCP* 39, 220–34.

_____ (1984): 'Irish kings and Bishops in the *Memoria* of the German *Schottenklöster*' in Ní Catháin and Richter (eds), *Irland und Europa: die Kirche in Frümittelaltes*, 390–404. Stuttgart.

Plummer, C. (1910): *Vitae Sanctorum Hiberniae*, i. Oxford.

_____ (1915): 'The miracles of Senan' in *ZCP* 10, 1–35.

_____ (1922): *Bethada Náem nÉrenn: Lives of Irish Saints*, ii. Oxford.

Power, P. (1914): *The Life of Declan of Ardmore and the Life of Mochuda of Lismore*. (Irish Texts Society, 16). London.

_____ (1932): *Crichad an Chaoilli*. Cork.

Power, D. (1994): *Archaeological inventory of Co. Cork*, ii. Dublin.

_____ and Lane, S. (2000): *Archaeological inventory of Co. Cork*, iv. Dublin.

Rees, A. and B. (1961): *Celtic heritage: ancient tradition in Ireland and Wales*. London.

Ryan, J. (1931): *Irish monasticism: origins and early development*. London.

Schreck, A. (1984): *Catholic and Christian*. Ann Arbor.

Sharpe, R. (1979): 'Hiberno-Latin *laicus*, Irish *láech* and the Devil's men' in *Ériu* 30, 75–92.

____ (1991): *Medieval Irish saints' lives.* Oxford.

____ (1992): 'Churches and communities in early medieval Ireland: towards a pastoral model' in Blair, J., and Sharpe, R., *Pastoral care before the parish,* 81–109. Leicester.

Sheehy, M. (1962): *Pontificia Hibernica,* i. Dublin.

Stokes, W. (1868): *Cormac's Glossary.* (Irish Archaeological and Celtic Society). Calcutta.

____ (1887): *The Tripartite Life of Patrick with other documents relating to that saint,* 2 vols, (Rolls Series). London.

____ (1890): *Lives of saints from the Book of Lismore* (Anecdota Oxoniensia). Oxford.

____ (1895a): *Félire hÚi Gormáin: The Martyrology of Gorman.* (Henry Bradshaw Society, 9). London.

____ (1895b): 'Cóir Anmann' in *Irishe Texte* iii, 285–444.

____ (1897): 'Cuimmín's poem on the saints of Ireland' in *ZCP* i, 59–73.

____ (1905): *Félire Oengusso Céli Dé: The Martyrology of Oengus the Culdee* (Henry Bradshaw Society, 29). London.

Swan, L. (1985): 'Monastic proto-towns in early medieval Ireland: the evidence of ariel photography, plan analysis and survey' in Clarke, H.B., and Simms, A. (ed.), *The comparative history of urban origins in non-Roman Europe,* ii, 77–102. Oxford.

Sweetman, H.S. (1886): *Calendar of documents relating to Ireland, 1302–1307.* (Rolls Series). London.

Theiner, A. (1864): *Vetera Monumenta Hibernorum et Scotorum.* Rome.

Thurneysen, R. (1933): 'Colmán Mac Lénéni und Senchán Torpéist' in *ZCP* 19, 193–209.

Thurston, H., and Attwater, D. (1941): ed., *Butler's Lives of the saints,* iii. London.

Todd, J. (1864): *The Martyrology of Donegal: a calendar of the saints of Ireland* (Irish Archaeological and Celtic Society). Dublin.

____ (1867): *Cogadh Gaedhel re Gallaibh: The war of the Gaedhil with the Gaill.* London.

Wagner, A. (1882): *Visio Tnugdali.* Erlangen.

Walsh, M. and Ó Cronín, D. (1988): *Cummian's Letter de Controversia Paschali and the De Ratione Computandi.* Toronto.

Walsh, P., (1918): *Genealogiae Regum et Sanctorum Hiberniae by the Four Masters.* Dublin.

Watt, J. (1972): *The church in medieval Ireland.* Dublin.

Wilkins, D. (1737): *Concilia Magnae Brittaniae et Hiberniae* I. London.

Zajac, Cronin and Kiely (1995): *Urban archaeological survey, Co. Cork.* Cork.

Index

of proper names, authors and editors

In general, except in the case of the most popular saints, the form used is saint's first name and principal foundation. *See also under* St.

Abbreviations used in this index.

c. county.   Used only for places outside of Co. Cork.

p. parish.   Used only where several distinct places bearing the same name occur or where the occurring name is the lessor known.

r. river.